DEVELOPING SUCCESSFUL
SPORT SPONSORSHIP PLANS

Titles in the
Sport Management Library

DEVELOPING SUCCESSFUL SPORT SPONSORSHIP PLANS

THIRD EDITION

David K. Stotlar, EdD

UNIVERSITY OF NORTHERN COLORADO

Fitness Information Technology
A Division of the International Center
for Performance Excellence
262 Coliseum, WVU-PASS, PO Box 6116
Morgantown, WV 26506-6116

Library of Congress Card Catalog Number: 2008938055

ISBN 13: 978-1-885693-87-7

Production Editor: Matt Brann
Cover Design: Craig Hines
Typesetter: Craig Hines
Copyeditor: Katherine Kline
Proofreader: Erica Reib
Indexer: Matt Brann
Printed by Data Reproductions Corporation
Cover photo courtesy of Kristopher S. Wilson/U.S. Navy. Back cover photo courtesy of Doug Haney/U.S. Ski Team

10 9 8 7 6 5 4 3

Fitness Information Technology
A Division of the International Center for Performance Excellence
West Virginia University
262 Coliseum, WVU-PASS
PO Box 6116
Morgantown, WV 26506-6116
800.477.4348 (toll free)
304.293.6888 (phone)
304.293.6658 (fax)
Email: fitcustomerservice@mail.wvu.edu
Website: www.fitinfotech.com

Table of Contents

Detailed Table of Contents

Chapter 4: Olympic Sponsorship Opportunities • 47

Chapter 5: Individual Athlete Sponsorships • 61

Chapter 6: Financial Implications • 75

Chapter 7: Developing Successful Sport Sponsorship Proposals • 83

Chapter 8: Securing Sponsorship Agreements • 97

Chapter 9: Managing Sport Sponsorships • 107

Preface

The third edition of *Developing Successful Sport Sponsorship Plans* was developed as a companion to *Fundamentals of Sport Marketing, 3rd Edition* (Pitts & Stotlar, 2007). This workbook evolved through several years of developing, reviewing, and critiquing sport sponsorships and draws on the author's experience in academia and the sport industry. While some discussion of sport sponsorship theory is presented in *Fundamentals of Sport Marketing*, this workbook examines the topic from the perspective of the sponsored property, rather than as a marketing tactic. It provides an overview of the theoretical underpinnings of the topic, followed by examples from actual sport sponsorships. In some cases, the name of the sport organization has been changed for reasons of confidentiality. Most chapters provide worksheets for use in constructing quality sponsorship proposals.

The intent of this book is simple: to provide a workbook that assists individuals in creating a sponsorship proposal through well-defined, industry-proven protocol. A sequential process is provided to build a quality sponsorship proposal that ensures success. Enjoy the workbook and good luck in seeking sport sponsorships.

Chapter One

UNDERSTANDING SPORT SPONSORSHIP

Introduction

Sponsorship, in its essence, is based on a mutual exchange between a sport entity and a corporation (Copeland, Frisby, & McCarville, 1996; McCarville & Copeland, 1994). This reliance on exchange theory suggests that both entities can simultaneously provide and receive benefits. Thus, a symbiotic relationship can be attained. In the case of adidas' sponsorship of the New Zealand All Blacks rugby team, Motion, Leitch, and Brodie (2003, p. 1083) noted "in sponsorship both the sponsor and the sponsored activity become involved in a symbiotic relationship with a transference of inherent values from the activity to the sponsor." In the United States and many other nations, sport organizations have aggressively marketed themselves to sponsors in an effort to obtain the funds necessary to operate programs. Seaver's research with 50 of the top U.S. sponsors indicated that 10% of sponsoring companies get more than 1,300 proposals per year (Seaver, 2004). 2008 North American sponsorship spending was projected to reach $16.78 billion, up 12.6% over 2007. Contributing to this total were several companies that spent over $100 million each on sponsorship programs (IEG, 2007). Among the top spending corporations:

> $330–335 million—Anheuser-Busch
> $305–310 million—Pepsi
> $230–235 million—General Motors
> $225–230 million—Coca-Cola
> $225–230 million—Nike
> $175–180 million—Miller
> $150–155 million—Daimler Chrysler
> $140–145 million—Ford
> $115–120 million—McDonalds
> $110–115 million—MasterCard

The major areas of the economy where sponsorship spending is apportioned have been noted below (IEG, 2007):

> Sports—69%
> Entertainment and Tours—10%
> Cause Marketing—9%
> Arts—5%
> Festivals/Fairs—4%
> Associations and Member Organizations—3%

Financial expenditures on sponsorship activities were not limited to North America. International corporate spending also escalated in 2007 as European corporations contributed $11.7 billion in sponsorship deals. In one very prominent example, Manchester United, the world-renowned British soccer club, announced it signed a jersey sponsorship deal with American International Group, Inc. (AIG) valued at $99.3 million for four years, or $24.8 million annually. The AIG deal succeeded the team's previous sponsorship with Vodafone Group, which ended its contract shortly after a change in team ownership. Along with topping the $16 million-a-year Vodafone deal, AIG's new sponsorship far outweighed a five-year, $88 million sponsorship that was signed by soccer rival Chelsea with Samsung (IEG, 2007).

Pacific Rim countries accounted for $9.5 billion with Central and South America spending an additional $3.5 billion. Various other regional spending accounted for $2 billion, bringing the worldwide 2008 total to $43.5 billion. With an increase of 14.8% above 2007 revenues, it seems sponsorship presents an opportunity for the growing list of multinational companies (IEG, 2007).

There is an increasing need for sport administrators and managers to understand the methodologies of this marketing component. Sponsorship has been defined as "a cash and/or in-kind fee paid to a property (typically sports, arts, entertainment, or causes) in return for access to the exploitable commercial potential associated with that property" (Ukman, 2004a, p. 154).

Some concerns exist as to whether the sports sponsorship field is saturated or if it will continue to grow in the years ahead. Many sports are heavily engaged in sponsorship (e.g., professional football, basketball, tennis, and golf) while others are less involved. From high school sports to college programs to professional leagues, everyone seems to want to be involved in sport sponsorship. The potential is so great that the Los Angeles Unified School District conducted a workshop for potential sponsors, and the Carroll Independent School District in Texas hired a full time director of sponsorships. San Antonio opted to hire an agency with the school district keeping 35% of the revenues ("A Tale of Two Districts," 2003). High schools in Texas and North Carolina went so far as to pursue naming rights for their facilities, a practice once reserved for professional teams. One high school near the Dallas-Fort Worth airport secured $4 million from Dr. Pepper to place a logo on the school's roof to be be seen by airline passengers (Popke, 2002). Another, Northwest Independent School District-Justin, erected a $1 million scoreboard in 2006 with space for 16 sponsors. At the collegiate level, about 10% of income for the National Collegiate Athletic Association (NCAA) Division I programs comes from sponsorship revenues with the average sponsorship for an NCAA Division I institution at $1.13 million (Tomasini & Stotlar, 2003).

Professional sport leagues have been able to increase sponsorship revenues substantially over the years. Control over the league's sponsorship is continually a topic in owners' meetings. Many owners want to preserve marketing rights for the team while others, principally in small market cities, advocate league wide sponsorships where revenues are shared equally across all teams.

In an effort to minimize the overabundance of signage inside sport stadiums, some professional teams (e.g., Buffalo Bills, Portland Trail Blazers) began to segment their stadiums. This concept involved the development of sponsor zones, each dedicated to a single sponsor and extending from banners on parking lot light poles to entrances and culminating with field, court, and scoreboard signage inside the facility ("Buffalo Bills Look," 1996).

Park and recreation departments are also engaged in sport sponsorship activities. Beyond the longstanding traditions of sponsors for little league teams and outfield signage at the ballpark, some park and recreation mangers are exploring new ground. The City of New York (NYC) signed a sponsorship agreement naming Rollerblades as its official in-line skates. Through the arrangement, Rollerblades provided free skates for security staff and offered free skating and roller hockey clinics in various NYC parks. Rollerblades also received special signage on the sides of security vehicles in Central Park (A.R.C., 1998).

What initially attracted sponsors to sport is the ability to reach consumers in a less cluttered environment than traditional advertising (Cordiner, 2002a). The clutter in advertising is such that the average consumer is exposed to over 5,000 messages every day. Sponsorship had the potential to deliver advertising messages more effectively than established advertising channels. However, sport may now have become over-saturated. According to Amshay and Brian (1998), many sport events have become "cluttered with title sponsors, presenting sponsors, supporting sponsors, camsponsors, official product sponsors, pouring rights, licensing rights, ad nauseam. Clutter and dilution are in direct opposition to what sponsors want" (p. 23). Skildum-Reid (2007) noted that "the massive preponderance of signage is unwelcome. It is clutter, and interruption, that detracts from, rather than enhances, the audience's experience with the event" (p. 10). In a cluttered market, many sponsors are seeking alternatives to mainstream sport, moving instead to action or extreme sports. Not only have they found these markets less cluttered, but the events have a strong psychographic pull with 18–24 year-old consumers (Cordiner, 2002b).

Several authorities note that sponsors are changing their strategy for sponsorship. The emerging theme is fewer, bigger, better. Poole (2003, p. 14) said that sponsors "would rather spend more money on bigger properties than spread their sponsorships around to more numerous, smaller properties." In 2004, the Tampa Bay Buccaneers moved to a "less is more" stance for their sponsorship. Their goal was to reduce clutter and provide better service to their marketing partners by limiting the total number of sponsors. A similar trend was seen at the 2002 World Cup in soccer, where the number of sponsors was reduced to 28, 15 partners plus official suppliers and licensees, compared to 43 at the 1998 World Cup in France. Seaver's 2004 corporate survey revealed the same direction. One executive commented, "We are doing fewer programs in the coming year; however, the programs that we're staying with will be bigger and better" (Seaver, 2004, p. 19) Another said, "What we'll be doing, we'll be doing at a higher level. Big impact is better for us, we feel, than a lot of small sponsorships. This will affect the second-tier sports and the number of people we will be talking to" (p. 20).

The issue of clutter also affects the methods that sponsors choose to communicate with consumers. Researchers at an event in Holland found that some sponsors were labeled "un-cool" because their presence was too obvious, while sponsors that had relevant activation were perceived more favorably. According to Ukman (2003, p. 2), "there is a huge gap between how marketers want to reach people and how people want to be reached." Similarly, Dan Migala, author of the industry insider newsletter "The Migala Report," noted that sponsorships are most effective when they enhance the participant's experience rather than detract from it. Visiting with participants in the ING New York City Marathon, Dan found that they particularly liked the activation by Gatorade and Dunkin' Donuts, who provided refreshments during the event. UPS also enhanced the runners' experiences by having its Big Brown trucks deliver runners' personal belongings from the starting area to the finish line (Migala, 2007). Thoughtfully designed sponsorships can bridge the gap between interruption and enhancement.

Sponsorship Background

In the early history of sport marketing, sponsorship activities often served the interests of corporate CEOs—as if they were saying, for example, "Let's sponsor golf, because I like golf." This allowed company executives to mix socially with elite athletes and also to provide client entertainment activities. However, these rationales have almost disappeared in the modern era of sport sponsorship. Nevertheless, most major sporting events continue to provide hospitality areas where executives can meet with celebrity-athletes before and after the competition as part of sponsorship packages. Notwithstanding these possibilities, greater sophistication evolved after the 1980s and 1990s, with the introduction of philanthropy to sport sponsorship.

There has been a considerable amount of debate about whether companies engage in sponsorship activities for philanthropic reasons or for financial benefits. Moreover, an interesting new term was recently introduced into the realm of business management. "Strategic Philanthropy" has been defined as "a company's long-term investment in an appropriate cause that does measurable good in society while enhancing the company's reputation with key audiences" (Jones, 1997, p. 33). In 2004, IEG began conducting seminars called Strategic Philanthropy for its corporate clients. The seminars focused on "Leveraging Philanthropy with Marketing" and "Putting Hope and Heart into Sales" (Strategic Philanthropy, 2004). Social responsibility has been an aspect of corporate philosophy for many years and numerous sport causes have benefited as a result. Corporations have donated to many different programs, and through this corporate giving, they have assisted programs in art, sport, medicine, and culture. However, corporate motives must be examined.

Whether or not a company engages in altruistic philanthropy, research has shown that consumers are influenced by a company's charitable activities. It has been found that 14% of consumers sought out companies with viable corporate philanthropy programs and 40% saw a company's corporate citizenship as a tie-breaker when deciding which company to patronize (Jones, 1997). Research also shows that the overlay of a cause can lead to increased purchase intent if there is little difference between brands on quality and price. However, the positive effects of cause-related marketing appear to diminish as the difference in competing brands increases (Roy & Graeff, 2003). There are many corporations that tie sport and cause-related marketing together. Verizon Wireless sponsors a team of professional women cyclists who volunteer to give any winnings to HopeLine, Verizon's initiative to help victims of domestic violence. They also created a program through HopeLine and the Chicago Cubs called "Safe at Home," in which used wireless phones, handsets, batteries, and accessories from any carrier were collected at the Verizon Wireless kiosk/booth inside Wrigley Field and refurbished for victims of domestic violence. In addition, Verizon donated $25 for every double a Cubs player hit during the season to Cubs Care, which supports domestic violence shelters in Chicago, and Verizon served as the title sponsor of the Cubs wives' "Cubs Care" event that raised $100,000 for area shelters through an auction and photo opportunities with Cubs players. The Cubs community relations department also provided home-game tickets to clients and staff of 15 domestic violence shelters in Chicago.

While it may seem ludicrous, some corporate officers talk about "owning a cause" (Jones, 1997, p. 36), which sounds more like a marketing strategy than true philanthropy. But, according to Jones (1997, p. 34), "it [doesn't] take long for consumers to see these tactics as sales pitches thinly veiled in the guise of social activism."

Granted, there may be corporations that engage in sport sponsorship for truly philanthropic reasons. However, the record shows that charitable approaches have limited success in securing corporate sponsorships. Corporate self-interest has been considerably more viable as a motivation for involvement with sport sponsorship.

A closer look at the reasons why businesses would be attracted to sport is detailed in Chapter 3.

Some of the more prominent justifications reveal that sport is attractive to sponsors because it can provide a more cross-sectional demographic exposure as compared to other marketing avenues. The diverse demographics represented by many sport activities and events is crucial to corporations and, thus, to the creation of potential sponsorship affiliations.

Sponsoring sport often adds a double exposure for sponsors with on-site promotional activities and media coverage. For example, Tiger Woods appeared on the cover of *Sports Illustrated* four times within one and a half years after winning his first Masters. He also adorned the covers of *Fortune* and *Business Week* (Lombardo, 1998). One sport marketer commented that you can buy the back page of *Sports Illustrated*, but you can't buy the front.

On the other hand, not all sponsorship is positive or even intentional. For example, an interesting yachting incident occurred when a Finnish boat, which had secured a sponsorship agreement just one day before a major international race, obtained significant exposure for its sponsor by capsizing during the race. The overturned boat was in range of television and news cameras, and it appeared on networks and newspaper front pages worldwide, displaying the sponsor's name. Although it was not the type of publicity that the sponsor had in mind, people around the globe turned their newspapers upside-down to read the sponsor's name on the side of the boat.

There are some authorities that believe that sport has become overly dependent on corporate sponsors to meet expenses. Three examples show that too much dependence on sponsors could have disastrous effects. In China, an international badminton tournament was canceled when sponsors pulled out during Asia's economic downturn. Also, the Chicago stop on the Women's Tennis Association (WTA) tour was canceled when International Management Group (IMG) could not secure a title sponsor. Further evidence was seen when a planned Women's World Doubles Championship in Fort Lauderdale was called off because the potential sponsors withdrew at the last minute.

Dependence on sponsorship monies is also evident with colleges and universities reliant on corporations and sponsorship revenues for additional income. In 2008, the University of Nebraska pooled all of its sponsorship and media assets and signed a 13 year agreement with IMG. Including the sponsorship rights held by the athletic department, the total value of the 13 year package was $143 million (University of Nebraska Board of Regents, 2008). Nike has all-sport agreements with 20 top college programs, while adidas has deals with about 15, including Texas A&M University and the University of Michigan, which both switched in 2008 from Nike to adidas. The Texas A&M deal was reportedly worth $60 million in cash and merchandise with a $6.5 million signing bonus. Many educational institutions have realized the benefits associated with sponsorship deals, such as:

1. Free equipment
2. Stadium advertising
3. Supplements to coaches' salaries
4. Television revenues for regular and post-season games

Colleges and universities in the U.S. have realized profits in the millions of dollars from corporately sponsored football bowl games. The Bowl Championship Series (BCS) games payout figures have been staggering. For 2008, the per-team payout for the BCS Bowl, Tostitos Fiesta Bowl, FedEx Orange Bowl, Allstate Sugar Bowl, and the Rose Bowl were $17 million (Smith, 2007).

In an attempt to gain greater control over sponsorship, the NCAA, along with many professional sports teams, has imposed rules regarding the size of corporate logos that can be displayed on team uniforms and equipment because of overt commercialization. However, in a recent lawsuit against the NCAA, apparel companies questioned the NCAA's motives when the bowl game corporate sponsors were allowed to place logos that exceeded the legal size limits on uniforms during the post-season games.

Major League Baseball (MLB) also implemented rules about the size of logos on bats after the 1990 All Star Game when a player held his bat up to the camera to display its over-sized logo—a promotion ski racers have been known to do at the end of a race as well. The National Football League (NFL) and the National Hockey League (NHL) created significant controversy by controlling the display of logos on player apparel. Their regulations state that manufacturers must pay the league a fee for the right to display their marks during a game. Thus, an NFL player who has an endorsement deal (see Chapter 5) cannot display a corporate logo on his shoes if the shoe company has not paid the league a rights fee. To illustrate the height to which this controversy has risen, in 2007, the NFL fined Chicago Bears player Brian Urlacher $100,000 for wearing a hat with logos of Gatorade's, official sponsor of the NFL, competitor on the Super Bowl media day.

Major League Baseball has not operated without controversy in this area either. In 1998, MLB owners relinquished their rights to sign exclusive team agreements with uniform shoe manufacturers. Previously, each individual team could sign with a single company (e.g., adidas with the New York Yankees). However, in an out-of-court legal settlement, the uniform rights for all teams now reside with Major League Baseball Properties. In another control-oriented issue, the Baltimore Orioles attempted to stop three players from promoting Pepsi products because the team had an agreement with Coca-Cola (King & Bernstein, 1998).

The question at hand appears to be, who has the right to control player sponsorships, the player or the league? Similarly, the NFL has, for many years, packaged league-wide sponsorships. In 1998, the league was unable to negotiate a league-wide agreement with Coca-Cola and relinquished the soft drink category to the individual teams. As a result, Coke signed 16 individual teams compared to Pepsi's three, while other teams remained without a soft drink sponsor. Thus, Coke was able to reduce its NFL sponsorship costs to $4 million, as opposed to the league-wide costs of $15 million from the previous year. In addition, Coke was able to select strategic markets where the sponsorships would be most effective. Unfortunately for many teams, their income was less than it had been in the preceding year (Bernstein, 1998a). As a result, Pepsi signed on as a "League" sponsor, securing rights to the Super Bowl. The league also created two new categories that teams could also sell—"Quick Serve Restaurant" and "Pizza."

Creating Win-Win Strategies

Sports activities and corporations can create symbiotic relationships that are greater than the sum of the separate entities. Ukman (2004b, p. 2) reported that "combining the assets of allied organizations creates sponsorship platforms in which the whole is worth more than the sum of the individual parts." Sport managers want to increase their revenues and the exposure of their programs. Coincidentally, sport sponsors want to increase their revenues and the exposure of their products. A sport sponsorship arrangement can fulfill these needs for each organization. Kim Skildum-Reid (2008) goes one step further and recommends a win-win-win protocol, which includes not only the sponsors and the organization but the consumer (participant or spectator) as well. In general, corporations are interested in marketing their products and services to potential customers. If sport can provide a vehicle for this endeavor, then a successful relationship can be established. The task for the sport marketing professional is to make it clear to the sponsor just how this can be accomplished through the organization or event. It is also critical that sponsorships enhance the experience of the participants and spectators, not detract from it.

Not everyone agrees that involvement with corporate sponsorships is beneficial for sport. Sport marketers should, therefore, be aware that not all members of the community embrace their involvement with certain corporate sponsors. Many feel that blending alcohol and tobacco with the healthful benefits of sports is hypocritical; as a result, there have been several moves on the part of government entities and regulating bodies to restrict alcohol and tobacco advertising in sport settings.

TOBACCO AND ALCOHOL SPONSORSHIP

Considerable debate surrounded a European Union ban on tobacco advertising in sport. The French government has had a ban in place for many years and has been pushing the application of legislation throughout Europe. The restrictions on tobacco sponsorship in sport vary across Europe. While a ban in the United Kingdom went into effect in 2006, the German government contended that smoking was a health issue and, therefore, should be within the control of individual nations ("Germany to tangle," 1998). Most of the alcohol and tobacco sponsorships have eroded in Europe, although the heavy dependence of Formula One racing on tobacco sponsorship has been an exception. This has led some organization executives to plan for races at venues in countries more sympathetic to tobacco advertising (Currie, 2004). Formula One was at the center of the controversy following the French government's ban on tobacco advertising in sport events. In retaliation to the ban, Foreign Intelligence Surveillance Act (FISA) officials dropped the French Grand Prix from its schedule of events because the French Auto Sports Federation could not guarantee that police would not impound cars and equipment displaying tobacco advertising.

The Australian government adopted legislation to restrict tobacco advertising, but the regulations allow events of "international significance" to apply for an exemption. The Canadian government also enacted legislation that restricted the display of tobacco advertising in sport. As of June 1998, sport and cultural groups got a five-year reprieve from the government's tough tobacco advertising restrictions (Danylchuk, 1998). Existing signage would be allowed to remain through 2000, and from 2000–2003, advertising by tobacco companies was limited to on-site displays and relegated to the bottom 10% of the sign (Danylchuk, 1998).

The French, Canadian, and Australian governments are but a few of those taking action on the issue. There may be many more in waiting, including measures in the United States resulting from a settlement between various states and the tobacco industry that addressed payments for medical coverage for smokers.

In 1991, the Federal Trade Commission (FTC) entered the debate surrounding tobacco and sport sponsorship. The case, *Federal Trade Commission (FTC) v. Pinkerton Tobacco Company* (1991) may have substantially changed the rules of the sport sponsorship game for tobacco companies. In this case, the FTC joined the battle to enforce a Federal Communication Commission (FCC) ban on television advertising of tobacco products. The case involved Pinkerton Tobacco Company's use of sporting events to advertise its "Red Man" brand smokeless tobacco. The results of the case yielded "cease and desist" orders outlining the methods used by Pinkerton, which were determined to be in violation of FTC and FCC regulations. Furthermore, it prohibited them from producing "program identifiers which appeared at the beginning or the end or before or after commercial breaks [that] include the Red Man Indian head logo" (*FTC v. Pinkerton Tobacco Company*, 1991, p. 329). The ruling also prohibited the use of a brand name of a smokeless tobacco product as the name of a sponsored event if "the logo, selling message color, or design feature of the product or its packaging" was used. Other restrictions included a ban on the use of the above-mentioned advertising on signage in areas which cameras routinely focus, such as on arenas, stadiums competing vehicles or other equipment, or on clothing of event officials, commentators, competitors, or participants. Furthermore, Pinkerton would "be liable for civil penalties in the amount provided by law for each violation of the order" (*FTC v. Pinkerton Tobacco Company*, 1991, p. 329).

Marlboro brand cigarettes and other tobacco companies successfully avoided television bans on tobacco advertising by purchasing advertising locations in numerous stadiums and racetracks that appeared in the background of televised events. Cigarette companies have had ads in numerous major league stadiums in the United States. At Fenway Park in Boston, the Marlboro sign hung in right field along with a sign for the Jimmy V Fund cancer research charity. According to DeParle (1989, p. 38), "the networks have been perfectly happy to show an infield decked with Marlboro banners and race cars painted with Marlboro logos—while pretending that cigarette ads are still banned from the air." However, the Federal Trade Commission recently joined the assault to enforce an FCC ban on the television advertising of tobacco products. The FCC, through the U.S. Justice Department, issued a restraining order in 1998 prior to the NFL Super Bowl to restrict television coverage of cigarette advertising locations in the stadium that would have appeared as background for television cameras.

In 1998, several states worked toward settlement with major tobacco companies related to health costs resulting from smoking tobacco. Part of the proposed agreement restricted all tobacco sponsorship of sporting events by the end of 2001. Any sponsorship agreement in place prior to August 1998 could be retained but not renewed. Preliminary interpretation of the settlement "allows tobacco companies to tie into one series, event, or team sanctioned by a single organization (Landmark settlement, 1998, p. 1). Although not precluded by the agreement, R. J. Reynolds dropped its sponsorship of NASCAR's Winston Cup series in 2004; officials will make substantially closer inspection of the settlement. Definitions and restrictions are rather vaguely worded, and few details were specified regarding what a "brand" entails. In many foreign countries, although prohibited in the U.S. agreement, tobacco manufacturers have diversified their product lines to include logos of non-tobacco consumer products. This begs the question: how could you restrict Marlboro from advertising "Adventure Gear" in print and electronic outlets? The current U.S. agreement applies the same restrictions to consumer products if a tobacco "brand name" (e.g., Winston) is used but allows use of the parent corporation's (e.g., R. J. Reynolds) identity. The settlement also eliminates "brand" sponsorship of stadiums and arenas in the States covered by the agreement ("Landmark settlement," 1998).

The controversy of beer advertising has not been as well publicized. In 1998, Carlsberg Beer negotiated and signed a contract to become a sponsor of the XVI Commonwealth Games in Malaysia; however, public pressures from the predominately Muslim society led the government to intervene. As a result, government officials forbade the games' organizers from displaying any of Carlsberg's logos on event materials or exhibiting event signage during the competition. Carlsberg was compelled to file litigation to recover its expenditures.

VIRTUAL SIGNAGE

Virtual signage has been one of the recent developments that challenge both sport marketers and event owners. The technology behind virtual signage "allows a broadcaster to electronically insert an image—generally an advertisement—onto any one-color surface, including a playing field or boundary" (Bernstein, 1998b, p. 24). A variety of sport organizations allow for use of this technology, while others restrict or prohibit its use. The National Basketball Association (NBA) has not allowed virtual signage, yet it is used extensively in Major League Baseball (MLB) and the National Hockey League (NHL). The NFL is still developing a policy on the issue. Other sports have also explored the use of this new technology. World Wrestling Entertainment, the X-Games, and various professional tennis tournaments have readily implemented virtual signage. The controversy centers around control of the images that are presented on the field. Many facility owners convinced sponsors to purchase stadium advertising with the idea that these signs would be seen on television. However, with this technology, not only could existing stadium advertising be blocked out, but a competitor's advertising could be inserted via this computer technology. As one Major League Soccer executive commented, "The stadium takes a position that they have some proprietary interest in [virtual signage], our position is that they don't" (Bernstein, 1998b, p. 24). The San Diego Padres ran into a disagreement when the broadcaster of its games began selling virtual signage during telecasts of home contests. The following year, the Padres specified in their broadcast contract that the team, not the broadcaster, would have the rights to any virtual signage inserted into Padres' games (Bernstein, 1998b).

Another point of contention has been the inclusion of sponsor signage in video games. Electronic Arts (EA), one of the leading producers of video games, has used a marketing theme: "If it's in the game, it's in the game." Up to this point, they have included outfield signage in their MLB games but have taken the concept to a higher level in their X-Games Pro Boarder game. This interactive game for the Sony Play Station includes prominent on-screen graphics featuring event sponsor Mountain Dew. Similarly, sponsors of soccer's World Cup are very conspicuous in EA's World Cup video game. Another video game producer, Sierra On-line, made sure to get permission to recreate corporate logos for its NASCAR video game (Rovell, 1998). Many sport marketers feel that these actions present an excellent opportunity to market to children in an authentic environment. EA Sports Director of Sports Marketing commented that "video games are a perfect vehicle for companies to target an attentive teenage audience" (EA Sports, 1998). There are, however, others who believe that this step represents another intrusion into the society that is unconscionable.

In summary, the relationship between sport organizations and sponsors must include advantages for both parties. This win-win situation can provide market value and higher profits for corporations and increase operating revenues for sport organizations and events. An overall view of the sponsorship process is provided in the Best Practice section that follows. The task for a sport marketing professional is to make it clear to the sponsor just how this can be accomplished through a particular sport organization or event.

BEST PRACTICE

Sponsorship Evaluation Model

The worksheets provide a guide to developing various sections of a sponsorship plan. The following sheets cover possible corporate rationale for sponsorship, legal restrictions, and controversies. Complete this worksheet as you would prepare a sponsorship plan.

Determine possible rationale that corporations may possess for sponsoring your team, organization, or event.

_____
_____
_____
_____
_____
_____
_____
_____
_____
_____

Discuss any legal restrictions (e.g., tobacco and alcohol laws) that would affect the sponsorship of your team, organization, or event.

_____
_____
_____
_____
_____
_____
_____
_____
_____
_____

Consider any possible controversies that may influence the sponsorship of your team, organization, or event.

_____
_____
_____
_____
_____
_____
_____
_____
_____

Chapter Two

PROSPECTING FOR SPONSORS

Identifying Sponsors

Involvement with sporting events and sports organizations is not the right partnership for everyone. In an off-handed comment at a national forum on sport sponsorships, one presenter made light of legal troubles incurred at the 2002 Winter Olympic Games by joking that a law firm should become the official legal counsel for the International Figure Skating Federation. Some things don't always fit. On the other hand, 2004 marked the first year that the Super Bowl named an official law firm—Winstead, Sechrest, and Minick, who worked with the Houston organizing committee during the bidding process and even into contract negotiations with the league and vendors.

Not all businesses in a community have the ability or the interest to buy into sport sponsorships, but some companies naturally fit with sport sponsorship. For example, San Francisco-based Gap apparel maker sponsored outfield signage to the left and right of center field, known as the "gaps" in baseball. Another natural match was evidenced by sport marketers with some creativity. Coming off a successful year in football, Colorado State University, whose mascot is a Ram, acquired Dodge trucks as a sponsor of their coach's show. Gatorade, developed in 1965 by University of Florida doctors to help re-hydrate their football players, has been a staple on NFL and college sidelines for 35 years. When the television audience sees a Gatorade cooler on the field, they know that the product works. Pepsi, owner of the Gatorade brand, extended its sponsorship with the NFL through 2011.

Sport marketers can find those businesses that have both the interest and the ability to participate. Sponsorship pioneer David Wilkinson said, "Make no mistake. The process of finding sponsors and then showing them how you can help them requires imagination and marketing effort" (1986, p. 40). As a starting place, sport marketers research the current trends within individual business sectors. Articles and trade publications are often great sources of information on corporate activity. Simply reading the business section of a local paper is a convenient place to begin. If dealing with the prospect of national sponsorships, the nation's leading business sources, like the *Wall Street Journal*, are useful resources. Looking for information on corporate mergers, business expansion, and product launches can be profitable. When financial services giant Wachovia merged with First Union bank in 2001, they embarked on a massive sponsorship campaign across the northeast and secured a variety sponsorship rights and teams deals as a result. Through the merger, the First Union center in Philadelphia became the Wachovia Center. In 2004, package and express delivery firm DHL was expanding its network across the U.S. Long known for its international services, DHL aimed at stealing market share from its competitors FedEx and UPS. They struck a deal with the United States Olympic Committee (USOC) just prior to the 2004 Athens Olympic Games and, through that association, bought exclusive advertising packages on NBC during the Games.

In another example, the Boston Marathon brought in the Mercedes Group for the 2004 race and its launch of the "smart" brand. The race offered substantial media exposure and 500,000 on-course spectators. Smart brand executives noted, "Smart drivers have a lot in common with marathon runners. They are more active than average and have a variety of interests. They have a zest for life, a great deal of enthusiasm and do not define themselves by age and social background, but by intellectual and creative potential. The smart brand will offer products that appeal to this audience in the United States" (Smart brand vehicles, 2004). Noting business activity like this certainly adds to the possibilities of finding sponsors who could benefit from a sport marketing platform. Other examples were evident in 2004 when Atlantic Coast Airlines re-branded itself as Independence Air. The Washington Redskins (NFL) secured Independence Air as a sponsor to help them communicate their new name and to promote their east coast routes (Ukman, 2004).

Access to this type of information also comes through sport sponsorship trade publications. Trade publications in the sport business field, such as *IEG Sponsorship Report* and *SportsBusiness Journal*, are valuable sources of information. *IEG Sponsorship Report* regularly publicizes the most active categories involved in sponsorship, such as nonalcoholic beverages (where 44% of properties had one as a sponsor), automotive (with 35%), banks (30%), beer (29%), telecommunications (26%), specialty retail (19%), food (18%), and financial services (14%) (IEG, 2003). Therefore, companies in these economic sectors may be likely candidates to approach for sponsorship.

Castiglione (1989) indicated that the local Chamber of Commerce is also a good source of information for analysis, as it typically includes records such as business profiles covering personnel, financial bases, and company products. Other sources suggested by Wilkinson (1986) include looking through the telephone book, examining ads in the newspaper, and simply taking a drive through the business district to stimulate your imagination in an effort to create a potential match. Another technique that has proven successful is examining specific business relations of a sport organization or institution. There may be some natural relationships that would be strengthened through a sponsorship agreement.

Many times businesses that you collaborate with have a vested interest in your success. Perhaps the best example of this concept is the enormously successful sponsorship of Hendrick Racing by DuPont. Understanding the circumstances shows that Hendrick owns more than 90 automotive dealerships with over $3.5 billion in annual revenues. Each of these dealerships maintains a collision repair facility that purchases a massive amount of automotive paint. DuPont Automotive Finishes happens to be one of the leading retailers of automotive paint. Thus, Hendrick gained sponsorship of its racecar, driven by Jeff Gordon, and DuPont gained product sales and significant other benefits through the relationship (Hagstrom, 1998). In a similar move, Sherwin-Williams entered into a partnership with the Big South Conference as its official paint supplier. "The partnership will allow Sherwin-Williams the opportunity to claim a strong foothold in a League that spends a large sum on paint and supplies each year" ("Sherwin-Williams," 2004, p. 4). Although not specifically mentioned, the relationship allowed Sherwin-Williams access to the entire University system of all members of the Big South Conference, which includes students, faculty, and staff who also buy paint.

As a follow-up step, the reader should generate a list of businesses and corporations that assess the criteria delineated in Chapter 3. Thereafter, rank the potential for each business listed as a starting place for sponsor prospecting.

Finding the correct point of access is often difficult. Some retail outlets arrange their own sponsorship agreements, while, in other situations, sponsorships are administered from corporate headquarters. Many local businesses are affiliated with franchises and chains of similar stores (e.g., Pizza Hut, McDonald's, and True Value Hardware). If some cases, the marketer may need to go through the corporate headquarters for approval. This is not always a disadvantage as the main corporation may have more money to commit than does a local retailer, and corporate executives may be willing to utilize ideas to promote the entire company. Regardless of where the final decision is made, a sport marketer should always visit with the local franchise owner or distributor first. If a sport marketer attempts to find a sponsor without at least tacit support from a local retailer, chances of success will be diminished. The Coors Beer example in the Best Practice section at the end of this chapter shows how the costs for sponsorship on some ventures were set up on a cooperative, shared-cost basis (also refer to Chapter 8 for more detail on corporate access).

Before asking a corporate sponsor what their business objectives are, research the following questions:

1. What type of product or service does the corporation produce?
2. What is their marketing structure?
3. What are their general marketing approaches?
4. What types of programs are successful?
5. Where does the corporation stand in relation to their competition?
6. Have they used sports and/or events previously and, if so, was their experience positive or negative?
7. Who makes their marketing decisions?

(List adapted from Wilkinson, 1986)

One of the keys to success is the ability to investigate the sponsoring company. Do the homework! The first step in investigating a corporation is gaining access to their corporate literature, such as their annual report. Begin by requesting the annual report directly from the corporate office, though many companies also post their annual report on their website. The Securities and Exchange Commission (SEC) requires all publicly held companies in the U.S. with over 500 shareholders and $10 million in assets to file annual reports. Information in these reports can be accessed through the SEC's website (www.sec.gov) and through the Public Register's Annual Report Service (www.prars.com). These documents will tell a lot about the inner workings of the target companies. There are, however, many things that a company doesn't want the public and their shareholders to know that the sport marketer needs to know. For example, just knowing who holds what office is not enough; you must know who the power brokers are in the corporation. For this perspective, read clippings from area newspapers, or talk to people who do business with the company.

The process also involves a thorough investigation of the sponsor's business structure. A sport marketer cannot possibly convince a sponsor that they are working in a sponsor's best interest without fully comprehending the sponsor's business. The senior marketing manager for Gulf States Toyota said, "The most critical tactic for a property that wants to work with us is to show us that they understand our business. It would go a long way in my eyes to know that a property had talked to dealers and sales people before even talking to me" (Williamson, 2004, p. 5).

A sport marketer's research should also investigate corporate ownership. In today's business world, the complexity of ownership means that companies you may be approaching have strong national and international ties. Pizza Hut, Kentucky Fried Chicken, and Taco Bell were, for many years, owned by PepsiCo (they are now affiliate operations). Would McDonald's become involved in a sponsorship that also included Pepsi? This would most likely never happen because of the strong ties between Coke and McDonald's through their restaurant association and their Olympic sponsorship alliance.

In many instances, a sport organization's financial partners may also serve as potential sponsors. First USA Bank is the third largest issuer of credit cards in the U.S. with more than $1 trillion in business deals. Some organizations, such as the National Football League and Major League Baseball have successfully associated themselves with national banking conglomerates to issue Affinity Cards. These credit cards feature NFL or MLB team logos, providing increased incentive for their customers to choose a bank's card, while benefiting the sport organization or league. Through these partnerships, the sport organization receives a set payment per subscriber and a percentage of sales generated from card use.

As noted earlier, the search for sponsors can be demanding and involves significant hours of research and investigation. However, it can also be a lot of fun and present a challenge that could motivate the best and the brightest sport marketers.

Adolph Coors Company
Sports Sponsorship Criteria

Here are Coors' criteria and rules for the Sports, CO-OP Events, Regional Events, and Special Marketing areas within the Field Marketing Department.

SPORTS

To qualify for sponsorship with Sports, subject sponsorship must meet the majority of the following guidelines:

1. Rank highly on the beer drinker index survey—participant, spectator, and viewer.
2. Score highly on the sports calculus—a calculation encompassing everything from size of audience to amount of product sold and retailer involvement opportunities.
3. Affect the bulk of the Coors marketing territory via on-site appearances.
4. Fulfill expectations or guarantee national media coverage.
5. Make sponsored individuals known and respected as a "leader" in their sport throughout the Coors market area, including media and spectators.
6. Create unique sponsored events, which contain the possibility of Coors "ownership." They should be directed toward the target market and on the upswing in popularity, and they should provide the Coors distributors with an opportunity for tie-ins.
7. Lend the Sport to solid consumer promotion possibilities, especially outreach.
8. Lend the Sport to the process of continuity with meaningful reach, as well as optimal frequency.
9. Be controlled by a viable sanctioning body (e.g., NASCAR) that establishes or designates all events.
10. Ensure events of the sponsored party, known as venues, are competitive in nature.

CO-OP EVENTS (between Distributor and Brewery)

The following rules have been established by the CO-OP Administration to ensure uniform guidelines for all Coors distributors. These rules provide distributors and departments within the company a summary of the CO-OP Administration's operating latitude. Any questions not covered by these guidelines should be discussed with CO-OP Administration management.

1. Funding for programs must be shared on a 50 percent distributor/50 percent brewery basis.
2. Programs must have a minimum total cost of $1,000 to be considered for funding.
3. Programs must be in compliance with applicable laws and regulations.

4. Programs must conform to the company marketing plan, marketing strategy, and corporate image.
5. Programs must be submitted on the authorized CO-OP Event proposal with enough information to allow for thorough analysis and evaluation.
6. Program proposals must be received by the area sales manager at least 30 days prior to the program start date or 60 days if special graphics are required.
7. Proposals submitted after program completion may be declined.
8. Co-sponsorships with other beer companies are not allowed.
9. Use of Coors logo(s) for advertising, point-of-sale (P.O.S.), and merchandising items must be approved through the CO-OP Administration to qualify for funding.
10. Code 3 items associated with an event, such as special imprint streamers and banners, will be CO-OPed only after the distributor's Code 3 budget has been exhausted.
11. Funds should not be committed to programs that distributors would support in the absence of such funds. The intent of the CO-OP program is to encourage distributors' supplemental involvement to include, and go above and beyond, their local communities.
12. CO-OP Events will also participate in the following additional activities:
    a. Local trade shows
    b. Product/package introduction parties
    c. Free-standing hospitality at major sports events, excluding transportation, lodging, and tickets for retailers and beer. A minimum of 10,000 spectators at a sporting event—excluding fairs, festivals, show, etc.—is necessary to qualify.
13. The following will not be considered for CO-OP funding:
    a. Beer
    b. Direct mail
    c. Capital equipment
    d. Salaries, bonuses, and other benefits for Coors distributors' employees
    e. Sales incentive programs
    f. Dinners, banquets, and luncheons that are unrelated to an approved CO-OP event, including entertainment at those functions
    g. Gifts and donations, either money or goods
    h. Purchase of tickets by distributors for retailer use
    i. Transportation or lodging for retailers

REGIONAL EVENTS—Fairs and Festivals

1. For the event to truly be a major regional event, it should draw a significant portion (i.e., 20%) of its attendance from outside the host distributor area.
2. Minimum attendance of 200,000 people (or 40,000 per day if it is less than a 5-day event).
3. Program cost to Coors of at least $10,000.
4. Distributor participation at a minimum of 30% and a maximum of 50% of the total cost.
5. Events must receive regional media coverage, specifcially media coverage outside the event's metro area.

6. Beer sampling opportunities.

7. Priority states will receive preference, and the Sales and Brand will define priorities.

8. Non-sporting type events (e.g., fairs, festivals) will receive preference over sporting events (e.g., fights, runs).

REGIONAL EVENTS—Program Development

1. Regional—The program should affect a broad geographic area and population base.

2. Series—the program should execute a multiple number of events in different locations to be conducted either simultaneously or over time.

3. Expandable—The program should be expandable and executable anywhere in the Coors market area.

4. High Participation—The program should be open to "mass participation" involving large participant and/or spectator numbers.

5. Have Continuity—The program should have a potential for multi-year involvement and development by Coors.

6. Contract Executed—The program must be organized and executed by a bona fide professional promoter with whom Coors has a signed contract/sponsorship agreement.

7. Distributor Co-Funded—The program must be at least 30% after the program's first year (T & D) of implementation.

SPECIAL MARKETING

Special Marketing will research, evaluate, and develop opportunities that match the young adult's lifestyle and brand objectives. The following profile of the young adult target applies to both Coors and Coors Light.

1. Demographic profile

    Age: . . . . Primary target: LDA-24

    Segments: . . . . Non-college
    College

    Sex: . . . . Primary target: Male
    Secondary target: Female

    Marital status: . . . . Single

    Work status: . . . . (Ranked by priority)
    Blue collar, white collar (gray collar)
    Part-time, unemployed

    Ethnic composition: . . . . . . (Ranked by opportunity) Anglo, Hispanic, Black

2. Demographic segmentation—college versus non-college:

College	Non-college
LDA-26 (same mind set as LDA-24)	LDA-24 (25–29)
Male	Male (primary)
$8–12K year (blue collar influence)	$12–24K year

2. Demographic segmentation—college versus non-college:* *(continued)*

Single . . . . Single

Anglo . . . . Anglo

White/gray collar. . . . . Blue/gray collar

*It should be noted that Coors Brand planned to put emphasis on the non-college segment and Coors Light Brand planned to put emphasis on the college segment.

3. Psychographic profile—descriptors characterize college versus non-college young adults

College	Non-college
More likely to consume light beer	Followers
Direction oriented	Subject to heavy peer
More secure	Pressure
"Purpose in life"	"World owes me"
Party-women-music	Hedonistic
Somewhat serious minded (focused)	Anti-gay
"Live for today" (smaller degree)	Adventurous
Work hard, play hard	Smaller circle of friends
Self-centered	Macho
Health conscious	Not secure in self
Participant vs. spectator	Work ethic not important
Conservative (see limitations)	Cars important "Power symbols"
Not moved by TV imagery	Fantasism/escapism
Not brand loyal	Look for acceptance
Peer pressure (jocks, Greeks, campus leaders)	"Live for today" ethic Moved by TV imagery
Looking for uniqueness in life	Elusive
Takes safe choice	Party-women-music
Into high visibility items that identify self	Cynical

4. Activities/recreation:

College	Non-college
Intramural sports	Bar hopping
Parties	Hunting/fishing
Music (concerts, records, tapes)	Motorcycles/motor sports
Movies (high consumption)	Video games
Fraternities (B.M.O.C.)	Music (concerts financially restrictive)
Limited transportation	Movies
University sports (spectators)	TV-viewing at home
Entertainment within close locale	(MTV/rock videos)

Photography . . . . Spectator sports (index higher)
Skiing . . . . Y.M.C.A./recreation center-oriented
Playing cards . . . . Local team participant
Swimming . . . . (i.e. Golf, darts, softball,
Tennis . . . . bowling, basketball)
Bowling
Weight lifting
Boating
Camping
Jogging
Racquetball

The following are examples of criteria that Coors uses to determine the relevance of a sales opportunity:

1. To what degree does the opportunity appeal to a young adult lifestyle (see previously listed profiles)?
2. How unique are the events?
3. Can the activities affect large groups of young adults on a major regional and/or national level?
4. Does the opportunity involve a 3-to-1 young adult ratio?
5. What entertainment activities, such as music and comedy, are available?
6. Is there an opportunity for Brand dominance or ownership?
7. Are the programs cost effective and turnkey operative?
8. Are the activities fun and do they offer an escape from daily pressures?
9. Are the programs extendible through distributor efforts?
10. Are there cross-promotional opportunities available (if applicable)?
11. Do the events offer consistency and continuity within and between markets?
12. Is there an impact in a Coors marketing area where high concentrations of young adults reside?
13. Can the programs serve as vehicles for national and regional advertising and/or consumer promotion opportunities?

Sponsor Prospecting Worksheets

The worksheets provide a guide for developing various sections of a sponsorship plan and cover potential prospects for sponsorship. Complete this worksheet as you would prepare a sponsorship plan.

Compile a list of all corporations that do business with you.

_____
_____
_____
_____
_____
_____
_____

Identify corporations that may have an interest in or connection to sport through various information sources (e.g., newspapers and journals).

_____
_____
_____
_____
_____
_____
_____
_____

List specific candidates gathered from your Chamber of Commerce search.

_____
_____
_____
_____
_____

Report specific companies located from a review of the Yellow Pages or from drive-by trips through the community.

_____
_____
_____
_____
_____

Specify the most feasible point of contact for each potential sponsor that you have located.

_____
_____
_____
_____
_____
_____
_____

Chapter Three

IDENTIFYING SPONSOR NEEDS

Introduction

As noted in Chapter 1, sponsorship in sport has been predicated on exchange theory with benefits accruing for sponsors and sport organizations alike. This chapter addresses the needs of the corporation. A quintessential need for any corporation is to differentiate itself from its competitors via a competitive advantage. A successful sport sponsorship may be an effective mechanism in creating and sustaining that advantage (Amis, Pant, & Slack, 1997).

Sponsor Rationale

According to AT&T's vice president of advertising and communication, "It's no longer a world where company CEOs decide to sponsor their favorite sports at any cost. Sponsorships are business decisions that must go through the same profit and loss assessment as any other" (Graham, 1998, p. 34). This point was further reinforced by Michael Payne, former International Olympic Committee (IOC) marketing director, who said that "corporation bosses are increasingly having to justify their marketing investments to their shareholders and can no longer just say being associated with the Olympics is good for a company—they will have to prove it with hard facts" (Keeping the Olympics, 1997, p. 32). One of the best clarifications of what sponsors are looking for in their relationships with sport organizations was forwarded by Donna Lopiano (Reynolds, 1998, p. 30): "Sponsorships have to measure up on a performance basis in their ability to match the right demographic and psychographic targets, reach the appropriate decision makers and ultimately help move product or services" In the end, sponsorship consultant Kim Skildum-Reid (2008a, p. 8) best summarized the point by saying, "It's time to get over yourself! Sponsors don't want to align with you, they want to align with their target market. So stop making the proposal about your need, your profile, and your general fabulosity," she wrote in her blog. "Start by talking about how you are a conduit for that sponsor to really connect with—not just get in front of—the target market."

Corporate Criteria for Sponsor Evaluation

According to Ukman (2004a, p. vii), "Talk to any four sponsors of any property and you will find that, while they are sponsoring the same property, each is using sponsorship to accomplish different objectives." For example, banks may be interested in new customer acquisition and business-to-business (B–2–B) relationships, while automotive sponsors may be looking to showcase new models and drive floor traffic. The criteria used by sponsors in their evaluation of proposals have been discussed extensively in the literature. Many corporations have developed definitive criteria, while others are more subjective.

Perhaps the most comprehensive study of corporate criteria was Irwin, Assimakopoulos, and Sutton's (1994) initial foray into sponsorship research, which produced a useful model for corporations to evaluate sponsorship proposals. Their model presented an array of factors for comparison (Irwin, Assimakopoulos, & Sutton, 1994, p. 59):

Budget considerations	Event management
Affordability	Event profile
Tax benefits	Organizing committee
Position/Image	Media guarantees
Product-sport image fit	Legal status
Product utility fit	Governing body status
Image-target fit	Marketing agency profile
Targeting of market	Integrated communications
Extended media coverage	Extended audience
Immediate audience	Public relations/publicity
Competition Consideration	Sales Promotions
Competition's interest	Personal selling
Ambush market avoidance	Strategies
Level of Involvement	Type of Sponsorship
Title sponsor	Established
Major sponsor	New
Co-sponsor	Team
In-kind sponsor	League/Championship
Exclusivity	Event
Long-term involvement	Facility
Once-off	

Further research was conducted to test the validity of their model. They found that the factors that were rated as most important fit between sport image and product/service image, target market fit, demographic profile of the extended audience, demographic fit of the immediate audience, and opportunities for signage (Irwin, Assimakopoulos, & Sutton, 1994). Additional research by Thwaites and Aguilar-Manjarrez (1997) found that community involvement and enhancement of the company image were highly rated, as well. Their study also found that corporate hospitality and building trade relations were considered to be important factors for companies seeking sport sponsorships. In addition, a considerable amount of research has shown that market-driven objectives, such as increased market share, new client acquisition, new product awareness and on-site sales, have been cited as critical factors (Copeland, Frisby, & McCarville, 1996; Irwin & Sutton, 1994; Kuzma, Shanklin, & McCally, 1993). Stotlar's (1999) research and Seaver's (2004) study of 50 leading U.S. sport sponsors revealed that sales and market-specific objectives were considered the most critical components in a sponsorship partnership. Corporate executives rated three items above all other factors: the ability to create new customers, to increase sales quantifiably, and to tie-in to the current marketing strategy. Ukman (2008) identified the top five sponsorship objectives as follows: increase brand loyalty, increase awareness, change/reinforce image, and drive retail sales. Obviously, there is considerable agreement across the industry. Several industry-based examples are illustrated below.

Reebok expects certain sponsorship elements in its event sponsorships, including on-site and local retailer sales activities, product expos and new product sampling, promotions of their national account representatives, Reebok athlete clinics and autograph sessions, scheduled press receptions, course signage and banners, national network coverage, and hospitality/VIP accommodations (Rohm, 1997). Volvo, a long-time sport sponsor, forwarded additional thoughts regarding its sponsorship decisions. Through its ups and downs with tennis, Volvo felt that a company should make large investments: "The big investment gives much more brand name exposure and, at the same time, is relatively less work" (Volvo and Sport Sponsorship, 1990, p. 5). Volvo philosophy also indicated a long-term commitment for five to ten years was more beneficial.

One of the basic criterion involved in matching sport organizations with sponsors is to establish a demographic fit between the sport organization's participant/audience base and the target market of the sponsor. For instance, the out-board engine manufacturer Evinrude sponsors several fishing tournaments. The VP of sales and marketing said, "We are able to have a presence in front of enthusiastic anglers nearly year-round, and anglers are one of our most important markets" ("Evinrude renews," 2004).

Economic factors are also a key element in a sponsor-event match. Investment firm Charles Schwab & Co. signed on to sponsor the Professional Golfers' Association of America (PGA) Tour through 2008. Not only can Schwab entertain high-income clients through its hospitality program, but they also provide investment-related services to PGA players and staff. The match seems better than if they were to sponsor action sports where fans and participants typically have less discretionary funds to invest. Companies sponsoring action sports are often looking to capture the elusive young consumer in order to influence life-long brand loyalty. Age represents one of the demographic variables in which sponsors may be interested, but gender may surface as another critical factor. While some corporations focus on a predominately male demographic, "companies are waking up to the power of marketing to women" (Reynolds, 1998, p. 30). Selecting the right fit with the sponsor on this variable is equally important.

When addressing demographics, the sport marketer should be sure to elaborate on how a sponsor can benefit from targeting a particular group. For example, convincing a sponsor that the demographic composition of an event is a good match with the corporation's target market is only the first step. The sport marketer, for instance, can make their database available for the sponsor's use in direct mail marketing. The National Athletic Trainers Association allows sponsors to access its 20,000 bi-monthly emails, noting, "If sponsors want to get a message out, we want them to use every communications piece we have available" ("Five Key Factors," 2004, p. 3). When AT&T Wireless, Sunkist, and Ace Hardware sponsored Little League Baseball, not only did they get signage at tournaments and other promotional elements, they got access to Little League Baseball's database (Lefton, 2003). Similarly, Dick's Sporting Goods secured sponsorship with Little League Baseball in 2008 to capture expenditures on sporting goods from this lucrative demographic, which allowed sponsoring corporations to mail advertising messages directly to 3 million Little League players.

There has, however, been an outcry that these actions result in an over-commercialization of youth sport. In an effort to reduce such protests, the American Youth Soccer Organization performs direct mailing for sponsors so they can screen any potentially offensive material (Johnson, 1998; Dunn, 2004). Although access to a sport organization's database can make a proposal more enticing, it may be more ethical to limit sponsors' use of mailing lists to include only consenting adult constituents. Remember, their personal information belongs to them, not to you.

Understanding and affecting consumer psychographics, the attitudes, beliefs and feelings of consumers, is also important to companies engaged in sponsorship. In this light, the U.S. Army has been very active in a variety of racing programs sponsoring vehicles in both the National Hot Rod Association (NHRA) and NASCAR. The psychographic profile of those fans, and the ability to set up displays with Hummers, tanks and a climbing wall, further enhances its ability to attract new recruits. The Army also sponsors USA Rugby, a seemingly natural fit for the psychographic of rugby players. Another interesting match is handgun maker Smith & Wesson's past sponsorship of a NASCAR team and driver.

Loyalty patterns are also extremely important to sponsors: data have indicated "that about 73% of NASCAR fans choose the products of their sport's sponsors over others" (King, 1998, p. 9). In 2004, data showed that NASCAR fans were three times more likely to purchase a sponsor's product over a similar product from a non-sponsor (Drehs, 2004). Pitts (2003) also found high consumer loyalty in her study of Gay Games sponsors, determining that 68% of participants recognized sponsors and that 74% of attendees intended to purchase from sponsors. The gay and lesbian market represents a $22 billion sport market.

As one author noted, "It is theoretically possible to put up the money to sponsor an event, hang a big billboard at the event, and have that be the end of it. But any organization that looked on sponsorship in this limited fashion would be foolish indeed" (Hagstrom, 1998, p. 51). Poole (2007, p. 16) commented that "sponsorship partnerships are less about signage and more about returning value to the sponsors while enhancing the overall game experience." Sponsorship expert Kim Skildum-Reid (2008b, p. 7) said, "I'm not saying that you need to ditch all of your signage, just stop talking about it. The more effort you put into how-big-is-my logo and where-is-my-banner, the less you will focus on the truly strategic aspects of sponsorship." Thus, sponsors can profit from an array of benefits attainable through sport sponsorship. To complement the research findings in this area, additional cases are presented that highlight corporate objectives in commonly cited categories, specifically awareness, image, sales, hospitality, and employee motivation.

AWARENESS OBJECTIVES

Understanding sponsor rationale regarding awareness has a lot to do with television. Ehrlich (1998, p. 26) posed the question: "What do the 20 official sponsors and suppliers of the World Cup hope to get from their involvement? Not just exposure in front of 2.5 million ticket holders. They're after a piece of the 36 billion cumulative television audience." Similarly, PGA Tour events are after the "Tiger Factor," where television ratings and shares increase on average 21%, or about 2 million viewers, if Tiger Woods is in the tournament and contending for the title (Bloom, 2008).

An important aspect of sport sponsorship that cannot be overlooked for the coming decade is the aspect of globalization. In a world economy, companies may find it difficult to communicate to consumers in Zimbabwe or China, but a sport sponsorship can help cut through some of the existing barriers. For example, UPS, a worldwide sponsor of the 2008 Beijing Olympic Games, viewed it as an opportunity to deepen international business contacts and hoped to reap benefits from these contacts in future business dealings. Many corporations are also capitalizing on the international success of sports like the NBA where, not only do U.S. players now have high levels of global recognition, but the increasing percentage of international players in the NBA make their endorsements increasingly valuable. UPS extended its sponsorship activities for Beijing by also contracting with the Chinese Basketball Association to capitalize on the popularity of players like Yao Ming and Yi Jianlian. Another interesting sponsorship with global implications came in 2008 when language tutorial company Rosetta Stone hired Olympic gold medalist Michael Phelps as a spokesperson while he learned Chinese for the 2008 Games (Mickle, 2008).

The awareness objective can still be effective even if relatively few consumers know anything about the sponsor's product or company; however, it has been shown to do little for a company like Coca-Cola. John Cordova (1996), senior business manager for Coca-Cola, referred to event signage as "wallpaper." In the 1980s, Coke's advertising motto was "if it stands still, paint it red, if it moves, sponsor it." This "be everywhere" strategy has been replaced by "consumer activation." In addition, its internal research showed that stadium signage did not drive product sales. Coke found that there was not enough profit from in-stadium product sales to justify large sponsorship expenditures. Furthermore, even "pouring rights" in the stadium were of marginal value; Coke found that the ridiculously high prices charged by some sport concessionaires were being blamed on Coke (Cordova, 1996). A similar note was sounded by Miller Brewing Company's director of sport marketing when he said, "The strategy is much more than how much signage we get. Visibility is not the key for us. Everyone knows who Miller is, but we need inventory that makes the brand come alive" (Lauletta, 2003, p. 8).

Additional support concerning the tenuous value of awareness came from former Nike Marketing Vice President Steve Miller when he indicated that Nike did not factor exposure of its logo into sponsorship valuation. He believed that, if people didn't recognize a Swoosh, the famous Nike logo, before the sponsorship, they never would. With college sponsorships, Nike has been more interested in how much product the partnership could sell at retail. This was the underpinning of Nike's 20 year relationship (replaced by adidas in 2008) with the University of Michigan, the number one selling licensed collegiate brand. Nike secured sponsorship of sport programs at the United States Air Force Academy (USAFA) but not only for the television exposure garnered through the Air Force football team's televised games and bowl appearances. They were actually more attracted to the $5 million a year in merchandise sales through the USAFA visitor's center, 33% of which was based off of Nike products. Sport marketing executives Amshay and Brian (1998) summarized the issue stating, "Exposure has value, but it is hugely overrated" (p. 23).

IMAGE OBJECTIVES

A company's image is the sum of beliefs, ideas, and impressions held by consumers about the company and its products (Ries & Trout, 1986). Given this concept, research has shown that sport sponsorship can help shape an otherwise obscure corporate image, but it can do little to change one. Skildum-Reid (2008a, p. 5) says that "properties cannot give a sponsor an image that they don't authentically have. They can only support, extend, or underpin an existing attribute." This was exemplified when Kmart Corporation sponsored various PGA golf events in an attempt to elevate its image by tying it to an upscale event. The strategy was not, however, very successful. In 2008, Hugo Boss renewed its sponsorship of the Davis Cup in tennis through 2012. According to Hugo Boss director of communications Philipp Wolff, "Tennis perfectly conveys the qualities of elegance, success and cosmopolitanism embodied by Hugo Boss" (Hugo Boss renews, 2007, ¶4).

This component can be observed in a variety of settings. Rolex does not sponsor rodeo events and Wrangler Jeans does not sponsor yachting. McDonald's research (1998) supported the benefits of matching the image of the sport with the image of the corporation. His research confirmed that a sponsorship was more effective if there was a high level of congruence between the image of the sport and that of the company. He evaluated the concepts of perceptual fit around the terms "sophisticated," "rugged," "exciting," and "wholesome." His research concluded that the creation of a good perceptual fit between the sport event and the sponsoring company could contribute to brand equity for the sponsor (McDonald, 1998).

An excellent overview of the sponsorship of the New Zealand Rugby Union's All Blacks by adidas is provided by Motion, Leitch, and Brodie, (2003; see additional readings). Following the scheme forwarded above by McDonald, the key attributes of the All Blacks were determined to be "power," "masculinity," "commitment," "teamwork," "New Zealand," "tradition," and "inspirational" (Motion et al., 2003, p. 1087). "When adidas evaluates a potential partner they look for two or three matching brand values present in their make-up or in the style in which they take part in sport. The values of 'tradition' and 'New Zealand' were matched to the adidas value of 'authentic'" (Motion et al., 2003, p. 1087). The authors summarized that "adidas and the All Blacks brand values were compatible and connected at a fundamental level" (Motion et al., 2003, p. 1090).

SALES OBJECTIVES

Sales objectives include such factors as increasing the sales levels of certain brands and getting people to sample a product. In most of the recent research on corporate criteria, the sales factor ranks near the top of the list in important considerations for corporations looking to engage in sport sponsorship (Stotlar, 1999). Steve Saunders (1996), marketing vice president at Coors, said that the bottom line for a Coors sport sponsorship is always, "Does it sell beer?" To illustrate the point, consider the case of Coors' association with the Colorado Rockies baseball team. At Coors Field, Coors has a microbrewery from which it bottles and sells specialty beer in the stadium and the general market. It also sells a significant volume of beer during the 81 home games and other events at Coors Field. Within the same industry, Anheuser-Busch's VP for Sport Marketing Tony Ponturo (2002) said, "It's not our goal to be a sponsor, our goal is to sell our product."

In assessing the value of Coors involvement, Saunders (1996) added that the days of "playing calculus" are over. His reference to calculus explained how, in previous years, Coors has utilized a formula to calculate a summative value of X dollars for a stadium sign, X dollars for pouring rights, X dollars per impression (i.e., $.05 per spectator), and X dollars for title to the event. In Saunders's view, corporate valuation will be based on the ability of an event to sell beer on site, to increase market share, and to provide direct product profits through Coors distributors.

For many companies engaged in retail sales, floor traffic equates to increased sales. Therefore, in a very successful arrangement with Wendy's restaurants, the United States Association for Blind Athletes (USABA) created the SportMates program. Through this sponsorship, Wendy's would make a donation to the USABA for each designated combo meal sold. This promotion resulted in a one-month sales increase of 34.5% for Colorado Wendy's outlets and enabled Wendy's to raise $25,000 for the USABA. In another case, Mercedes-Benz sponsored ATP, one of the top professional tennis tournaments, and, as a result, was able to sell over 150 cars to tournament players alone. They also offered promotions in tournament host cities to create floor traffic and test drives. A combination of the two has proven to be a very successful maneuver for Mercedes.

adidas signed up with the Royal and Ancient golf course in St. Andrews Scotland as its official supplier. Not only does adidas outfit all of the staff during its tournaments, but it also has exclusive sales of apparel from the pro shop. Although the numbers are not available, it can be assumed that a large portion of visitors to the birthplace of golf would take home a golf shirt as a souvenir. Similarly, sportswear company Champion, owned by Hanes brands, signed up for title sponsorship of the Wide World of Sports stadium, part of the Disney World complex, to promote Disney. But they also saw an opportunity for exclusive sales rights to clothing sold at the venue, as well as all Disney parks and resorts.

Product sampling has also been an effective sponsorship tool by assisting sponsors in attracting potential consumers. USA Swimming and Johnson & Johnson's Sundown Sunscreen products implemented one such example; their sponsorship agreement provided that Johnson & Johnson send sample packets of sunscreen to over 2,000 local swim clubs for distribution at area swim meets. This met one of the primary objectives of the company—to get the product into the hands of the most likely customers; and who better than young swimmers and their families?

Product sampling continually generates a great deal of interest in the product, and sales can be tracked to indicate an overall effect on sales. It also has been shown to be effective in developing consumer loyalty and providing the company with reliable feedback on products with minimal costs.

Service companies can also generate sales through sport sponsorship. The New England's (insurance and investments company) involvement focused on tennis' AT&T Challenge stop on the ATP Tour. The results from its $50,000 sponsorship of the event generated 2,500 leads and over $200,000 in insurance sold. Here, sponsorship strategies are centered on effective sales objectives as the primary criterion. In addition, another sport executive also commented that the "focus should not be strictly on exposure, but [be] more sales driven" (Seaver, 1996, p. 33). According to a recent industry survey, a sponsor was quoted as saying, "It's real simple. Ultimately what we have to do is to sell product. A banner ad does not cut it. We need to know that our involvement sold something" (Seaver, 2004, p. 17). One director of sponsorships said, "We are no longer satisfied with enhanced image; give us opportunities for on-site sales . . . dealer tie-ins and we'll listen" (Seaver, 1996, p. 34).

Thus, the relationship between sport organizers and sponsors has evolved to accentuate "return on investment" (ROI). As a Worldwide sponsor of the Olympic Games, General Electric was able to use its business associations with the 2008 Beijing Olympic Games to secure $153 million in construction and infrastructure projects in its first two years of the sponsorship. Irwin and Sutton's research (1994) on corporate criteria found that market-driven objectives, such as increasing sales and market share, were highly rated as criterion in sponsorship selection. Calculated value assessment replaced other factors as the primary strategy employed by both event owners and sponsors during the 1990s and is a mainstay of sponsorship industry.

In support of this transition, the top ranked criterion in Seaver's (2004) industry survey was "a program with the ability to drive quantifiable sales into area retailers"—76% of participants ranked it as extremely important, and 20% cited it as important. Xerox personified this concept in its Olympic sponsorship campaigns by carefully tracking sales records, which revealed 35,000 leads and the sale of more than 6,000 copiers directly attributable to its Olympic strategy and marketing initiatives (Stotlar, 1997).

Reebok has also emphasized the sales aspect when it evaluates road-race sponsorships. They have prioritized events in which they can sell product at the race site or, alternatively, involve local Reebok retailers. In another example, the CEO of Ranger fishing boats, sponsor of several bass fishing tournaments, said sponsorship is not about delivering a million impressions but about getting the message to someone who is going to buy a $20,000 boat in the next 12 months. The clear message is that helping a sponsor move product can develop deeper revenue. Coca-Cola's Cordova said, "Bring me a promotion that will put a Coke in the hands of a 12 year-old and we can work a deal" (Cordova, 1996).

Both Coca-Cola and Pepsi have consummated countless sponsorship arrangements with public school districts, private schools, and colleges and universities across the country. In its association with Jefferson County School District in Colorado, Pepsi procured signage in 59 schools and on 10 school buses in addition to exclusive vending rights on school property. In return, each high school received $25,000, junior high schools were given $15,000, and the elementary schools made $3,000 apiece. Although some members of the community were opposed to what they saw as an over-commercialization of schools, the majority of citizens supported the sponsorship.

HOSPITALITY OBJECTIVES

Sponsors need places and events to use for entertaining potential clients and enhancing business-to-business relationships (B–2–B). Sporting events have, for many years, provided great opportunities for these activitie. NASCAR has been one of the more successful sports in leveraging its popularity through hospitality activities. First, all of the racetracks offer corporate suites in conjunction with sponsorship packages. At Darlington International Raceway, the suites have been priced at $200,000 and have attracted companies like Interstate Batteries, Pepsi, and DuPont. DuPont, which sponsors Jeff Gordon's racecar, typically entertains up to 2,000 clients, employees, and associates at a single event, taking them on tours of the pits, providing them a fabulous meal, and letting them visit with Jeff Gordon prior to moving up to their suite to watch the race. At the Colonial golf tournament, sponsor Bank of America brought in 1,000 of its top clients to its 13th hole skybox and invited 40 VIPs, so-called "high value" clients, to extend their stay and play the course the day after the tournament. Similar tactics were in place at the America's Cup sailing races where some sponsors hired yachts to cruise the racecourse while conducting hospitality events. Hospitality does not come cheap, however. At the 2005 US Open in golf at Pinehurst, a tent in the sponsor village started at $100,000 for 50 guests and went to $750,000 for a more sophisticated clubhouse location. These prices only include the space to entertain and typically do not provide food or beverage services.

Hospitably is often referred to as Business-to-Business (B–2–B) marketing. This is where businesses can develop relationships with their best customers. It's about influence and, what the industry refers to as, creating a "network" position. Compaq Computers uses its sponsorships to develop relationships and influence Information Technology (IT) decision makers in the nation's leading companies. According to Ethan Green, former sponsorship manager for Compaq, among the company's sponsorship criteria was the involvement of IT decision makers with the event. The company was less interested in influencing consumers to purchase low-end computers every few years than they were in targeting people who would make the decision to purchase computers, networks, and printers for major corporations (Green, 2002). In 2003, when Bank of American signed on as sponsor of the Colonial golf tournament, it wanted to improve the bank's relationship with its key accounts. They created "Hogan's Alley," which resembled a fine country club with conversation areas, food, and entertainment. Their research after the event showed that 73% of attendees thought it was the best corporate hospitality that they had ever experienced. More importantly, 84% said that the experience strengthened their relationship with the bank. FedEx uses its relationship with the NFL to provide hospitality events in stadiums on non-game days. These events provide controlled sales environments that capitalize on the draw of the team. They also give FedEx an experience that the typical fan cannot buy. "Hospitality is sponsorship and marketing at its best because it allows a company to achieve so many objectives" (Migala, 2004a, p. 4).

EMPLOYEE MORALE OBJECTIVES

One established method of increasing employee morale is to involve famous athletes in corporate affairs. Texaco has a longstanding association with racing's Mario Andretti and has invited him to serve as a motivational speaker in numerous corporate meetings. After his speech, Andretti would sign autographs, mingle with employees, and discuss the importance of hard work and attention to detail. Similarly, Xerox used 1996 decathlon gold medalist Dan O'Brien for corporate presentations prior to the Atlanta Games. Not only did this activity inspire employees at work, but it also gave them an incentive to watch the games and cheer for O'Brien.

VISA has also successfully used its Olympic sponsorship to build team spirit within the corporation. One of its techniques was to make Olympic logo golf shirts available to all employees. During the lead up to the Games, they had to reorder shirts five different times because of the high demand. Another Olympic Games sponsorship example occurred when John Hancock Insurance, now part of Manulife Insurance, utilized its worldwide sponsorship of the Olympic Games to motivate its employees. Sales staff responded to opportunities to win expense-paid trips to the Atlanta Olympic Games, and the company realized revenue increases of 50% in 1995 and 35% in 1996 (Kennet, Sneath, & Erdmann, 1998).

OTHER SPONSOR OBJECTIVES

Additional criteria upon which companies make sponsorship decisions include other current sponsors and mix of products, corporate relations with other sponsors, cooperation from the host facility for signage, access, and placement, and the potential for VIP contacts. An outline of the sponsorship needs examined by Anheuser-Busch is presented in Figure 3.1.

The number of events and their geographic representation are also key elements in sponsor decisions. The International Events Group has clarified the difference between national and regional events. Ukman (2004) indicated that, to be considered a "national" event, the sponsorship impact would need to affect 15 major markets. Otherwise, it should be classified as a regional event. Major companies that have national or international distribution channels are always interested in

Season Tickets	**Yearbook/Press Guide/Program/**
a. Complimentary	**Scorecard Ads**
b. Discount	a. Complimentary
c. Full purchase availability	b. Discount purchase
	c. Full purchase
Reserved Seat Tickets	d. Number of complimentary copies
a. Complimentary	
b. Discount	**Arena Signage**
c. Full purchase availability	a. Availability
	b. Number
General Admission Tickets	c. Complimentary
a. Complimentary	d. Charge (amount)
b. Discount	
c. Full-purchase availability	**Special Items**
d. Blocks for charity use	a. Use of VIP rooms
e. Scoreboard mention	b. Use of luxury box
f. Invitations	c. League/press passes
	d. Parking passes
Special Stadium Nights	e. Ticket purchase option
a. Free tickets	f. Use of highlight film
b. Special meeting room	g. Use of product music
c. Souvenirs/programs	h. Merchandising
d. First-ball ceremony	i. Sampling opportunity
Use of On-Air Talent	**Scoreboard/Public Address Exposure**
a. Lead-ins	**in Stadium**
b. Drop-in	a. Copy only
c. Live announcer	b. Copy and art
d. Special promo spots	c. Number of times per game
e. No charge	d. Complimentary
f. Charge (amount)	e. Discount purchase
g. Re-use off station	
On-camera	**Participation in Events**
Off-camera	a. Pre-Game
	b. Half time
	c. On-field or on-floor
	d. Presentations

Figure 3.1. Anheuser-Busch Sport Sponsorship Program

wholesaler tie-ins. This typically relates to the ability of a local distributor to have special promotions, on-site displays, and possibly cooperative advertising. Some corporations are also drawn to sport sponsorship by the potential for merchandising. Miller Brewing Company began selling facsimile jackets and t-shirts on the NASCAR auto racing circuit and, not only realized substantial profits from the products themselves, but increased its visibility and extended its influence into the local community for periods far in excess of the race day. UPS, for example, generated over $500 million dollars in sales of branded merchandise in the first month of the sponsorship of its NASCAR team.

The power of relevant activation cannot be overlooked. Sponsors need to communicate with each of the audiences in meaningful ways. Simply throwing up a sign and putting the sponsor's logo in the game program won't work. Coca-Cola uses its sponsorship of the Olympic Games to extend its reach into the community by also sponsoring the Olympic Torch Relay. Coca-Cola is more involved in communities by selecting local Coke bottlers to participate in nominating Olympic torch runners. In 2008, the first time the torch traveled internationally, Coke activated its sponsorship across China, Africa, and throughout the international route of the torch. Although the Torch Relay met with some international protest, based on China's stance on Tibetan independence, the local activation efforts were a success.

State Farm Insurance also successfully activated its sponsorship as an NCAA corporate partner with its traveling "Fan Experience" display at NCAA championship events and on college campuses. According to Liberman, "State Farm wants to reach college-educated young people who are on the cusp of making decisions on insurance for their adult lives" (2008, p. 22).

Coke used another activation strategy when it took over sponsorship of the NHRA with its PowerAde brand; as title sponsor, Coke wanted to connect with racing fans. It launched a special flavor of its sport drink called "NHRA PowerAde" after field testing and online research with NHRA fans.

In another Olympic-related sponsorship, VISA was able to activate its card usage through member banks by offering sweepstakes for trips to the Games. At one bank sweepstakes, every transaction with a VISA card qualified as an entry into the drawing, and as a result, bank revenues increased 300% over a control group during the 60-day promotion ("Staying ahead of the Games," 2004). At Turner field in Atlanta, sponsorship with the area Lexus dealers provides reserved parking for Lexus owners. BMW also activated its sponsorship with American Ski Corporation, owner of seven ski resorts, by supplying hotel guests with the courtesy of BMW sport utility vehicles—the program generated 15,000 test drives. At the higher levels, BMW invited 150 of its best customers for expense-paid ski vacations. In New Zealand, cereal maker Weet-Bix sponsored a face-recognition website where kids could go online and match a player on the All Blacks rugby team to their own faces (Skildum-Reid, 2008c). It was tremendously successful. These types of activation strategies bring the customer directly in touch with the benefits of sponsorship.

Industry data have shown that a lot of sponsors are not spending enough money on activation. Performance Research (2004) found that 70% of sponsors are spending less than the suggested $3-to-$1 on activation. The industry average was only $1.75 for each dollar spent. Former MasterCard Vice President of Global Sponsorships and Event Marketing Bob Cramer commented, "We are talking about activation with more and more of our partners. We are looking at activation like inventory, and properties need to do the same. It is a hard pill for properties to swallow because it is not so much about what they can do for us at the event but in the marketplace" (Migala, 2004c, p. 2). The sponsorship director for Janus commented about sponsoring the New York City Triathlon, "Half of the properties we work with expect us to create our own programs, pay for them, and implement them completely on our own. They want us to pay a sponsorship fee and they leave all of the activation up to the sponsor. In concept that might work, but in reality it usually doesn't. We have to do things in tandem to make sure things work smoothly" (Sponsors Identify, 2008, ¶1).

Activation also encompasses using sponsorship across the business, often referred to as integration. Cordiner (2002) noted that "brands need to integrate sponsorship across all business activity to make it work and the relationship between brand and sports property needs to be nurtured and developed over time to be truly effective" (p. 15). An example of integration was seen in Saturn's sponsorship of Arizona State University's homecoming activities. Not only did Saturn get vehicle displays and hospitality sites at all of the athletic events, but it received identification in football broadcasts and on 125,000 direct mail pieces that went out to students and alumni ("University reaps," 2003). Another example of corporate integration on sponsorship activities can be seen with the FedEx example in the Best Practice section of this chapter.

Another emerging activation follows the marketing trend of "experience marketing." Though sponsorship corporations are looking for ways to relate to their products and enhance their experience with the event, "sponsors will look for an individual, event, club, or organization in the sports arena that carries a sufficiently high level of emotional involvement with their target audience" (Cordiner, 2002, p. 14). Furthermore, "sponsorship must motivate consumers to interact with the sponsor's product—whether that's touching it, using it, speaking to a specialist about it, etc.—and have them walk away with more knowledge about it" (Product integration, 2004, p. 3). Green (2002) identified integration as one of Compaq's key elements in sponsorship screening. If the sport property does not integrate Compaq computers into the event, they are not interested. Thus, the Houston Marathon was able to secure Compaq as a sponsor by using computers to track runners on the course from the sponsor's on-site tent and through their website. These experiences will, in turn, increase consumer purchase intentions. Although including these elements creates added benefits, the situation should not be left to chance. The extent and level of integration should be formalized in the contract and should note the specific activities that will ensure success.

An excellent example of integration occurred in Nextel's sponsorship of NASCAR from 2004 to 2007. Nextel created "FanScan In-car Audio," a wireless service that connects fans with the live communications between drivers and pits during the race. "Nextel's affiliation with NASCAR is based entirely on how we can leverage our core competencies in wireless communication to enhance the fan experience . . . immersing them in the entire experience so that they are part of the action" ("Nextel launches," 2004).

Cross-Promotion

Cross promotion, the ability of sponsors to work cooperatively in a sponsorship, has been noted to be "among the most powerful and popular activation methods as they can grant marketers access to new distribution channels and spread out promotional costs across multiple partners" ("Five Key Factors," 2004, p. 3). In 2004, NASCAR put together a B–2–B Council to help sponsors work together more closely and to cooperate on a variety of hospitality and activation strategies.

The NHL's Phoenix Coyotes put together a deal with the team Coke and Fry's Grocery. Fry's, a primary Coyotes sponsor, offered the team control of the entry end-caps, the end section of each of the shopping isles, in each store as part of its sponsorship. Coke desperately wanted end-cap control to lure consumers to their product. To do this, the team arranged a promotion in which customers could trade in their Coke cans from Fry's to redeem a free kid's ticket for every adult ticket purchased. The cross-promotion produced increased floor traffic for Fry's, incremental sales for Coke, and sold Coyotes tickets. Coke cross-promotes its NASCAR sponsorship by partnering with primary sponsor Home Depot stores by featuring the Home Depot Team driver on its Coke machines at all stores.

The Coyotes also secured a cross-promotion arrangement with Budweiser. This deal provided for 18 Budweiser semi-trailer trucks to be outfitted with Coyotes' murals on the side. In covering their distribution routes, these trucks drove all over Arizona and New Mexico promoting the Coyotes hockey team 24 hours per day. Another successful cross-promotion strategy was created by the NHL's Florida Panthers in 2008. They developed a "partner-only" website where its business partners could network and work on promotions among themselves, increasing the value of the involvement with the team (Talalay, 2008).

In the sport of fishing, sponsors of a series of fishing tournaments banded together to package their products for participants and spectators that included Evinrude out-board motors, Ranger fishing boats, and Everstart Marine Batteries in the "Ultimate Fishing Package" ("Evinrude renews," 2004). In another cross-promotion, Olympic partner Coca-Cola persuaded one of the athletes it sponsors, 2004 Olympic wrestler Shane Hamman, to spend a day at fellow sponsor 24 Hour Fitness working out with a lucky employee and gym member who won an in-store contest. As part of the contest, 24 Hour Fitness, in turn, promoted Coca-Cola's PowerAde line of sports drinks.

Sponsors are also motivated by the type and amount of press coverage, both print and electronic, which they receive as a result of the sponsorship. Sport organizations can utilize data collected from previous events, or from similar events if a new event is proposed, to convince sponsors there is a sufficient media value returned through the sponsorship program. The data could include column inches that appeared in the newspaper and airtime of news or special reports related to the event on television and radio.

The timing of an event can also play an important role in sport sponsorship. Companies continually introduce new products and services to the market. A growing number of cruise lines are using sport sponsorship to promote new cruise activities, like climbing walls and adventure side-trips. Airlines are adding new cities to their routes, and tying an event into a new destination can prove to be advantageous for the airline. In addition, seasonal timing should be examined. Automobile dealers typically introduce the new model year in the fall, which coincides with football season, and could create a great opportunity for new products to be displayed at games. In another example, computer game maker EAS has sponsored the Maui Invitational basketball tournament. This tournament has featured the nation's top collegiate teams and falls at the beginning of the holiday shopping season in late November. Circumstances like these create enormous opportunities for sport marketers, as new companies look for effective strategies to promote their new identity.

Details surrounding an event's organizing committee are also important to potential sponsors. The event organizers should be well prepared and financially stable with a proven record of organizing other activities. Sponsors are always going to be cautious about lending their name and corporate identity to another entity; therefore, attention to stability and professionalism is imperative.

Sponsors are also wary of the multitude of risks that may be associated with an event. The potential for a public relations disaster should be tolerable. There are always risks, some dealing with the weather, but the organizers should be willing to point out potential risks to the sponsor. One specific example illustrates this point. When Dodge trucks became involved in the sponsorship of the Iditarod, a major dog sled race, they were unaware that the public relations generated from animal rights activists could produce a substantial amount of negative press coverage and controversy. Similar risks can be found with rodeo events. As a preemptive maneuver to offset such a controversy, the Professional Rodeo Cowboys Association published a brochure on the protections and humane treatment of animals that sponsors can use to explain the activities and defend its events.

Sometimes even the type of sponsorship can cause controversy. In 2004, the Daytona Cubs, a Triple A baseball team, conducted a funeral give-away to the best essay on a fan's ideal funeral. The program was sponsored by a local funeral home but caused many in the community to be upset over what they considered to be the trivialization of death ("Baseball's Cubs run free funeral promotion," 2004)

Cause-Related Sponsorship

One of the most significant trends in sport marketing is to affiliate a sport sponsorship with a popular cause. Muellner (1998) noted, "Without a doubt, there are a lot more companies trying to market with cause-related endeavors" (p. 8). The rationale for involvement in cause-related marketing is clear when a more detailed look at consumer response is considered. Irwin, Lackowitz, Cornwell, and Clark (2003, p. 138) noted that "it is critical that the CRM [cause-related marketing] tie-in be viewed as valuable and genuine to the consumer. They noted that 83% of consumers developed a more positive impression of companies engaged in CRM." Several examples of this practice can be detected throughout the sport industry (also refer to Chapter 1).

Started in 1996, an event was developed to honor the late college basketball coach Jim Valvano and raise money for cancer research. The college basketball tournament entitled "Coaches vs. Cancer" raises over $1,000,000 each year. Another example is the Terry Fox Run to raise funds to fight cancer, which began in 1995. This event has been held in 53 countries and has been one of the most ambitious international cause-related sporting events. Furthermore, Race for the Cure represents another very popular running event held annually in numerous communities across the U.S.

to raise money for breast cancer research. Race for the Cure raises over $60 million annually; the majority of which stays in the host communities.

"Studies support the notion that consumers feel better about a brand they believe is contributing to society" (Muellner, 1998, p. 8). An IEG sponsorship report (Ukman, 2004) indicated that "nearly half of Americans are engaged in some form of consumer activation" causing buying decisions to rest on the social actions of the companies from which they purchase products (p. 2). Furthermore, "the more affluent the consumer, as well as the more highly-educated, the more they participated in consumer activism" (p. 2). Their research also showed that 78% of consumers would buy from a sponsoring company that was associated with a worthy cause about which they cared. In addition, 66% reported they would switch brands, 62% would switch retailers, and 54% said they would pay more (5–10%) for items offered by a company that was involved with an important cause (Ukman, 1997, p. 2). Consumers were equally perturbed at companies that lacked a viable philanthropy program. More than 50% of consumers had actually boycotted products from companies that were not active in social programs. Despite all of the success, some degree of caution must be exercised in cause-related marketing campaigns. One marketing executive noted, "If something is done purely for publicity, people see through it— it has to come from a motivation to work for the betterment of the community" (Muellner, 1998, p. 8).

Grassroots (Community-Based) Sponsorship

Grassroots sponsorship brings marketing to a local community or region, as opposed to a national scope. Pepsi modified its strategy for multicultural sport marketing in 2004 by opting to spread its dollars across a greater number of small events with focused ethnic profiles ("Pepsi wants," 2004). Previous research has shown that several factors evident in national sponsorship selection were the same as those for sponsoring grassroots sport; most notably, increasing corporate exposure and consumer awareness were present in both national and local sponsorship. Another advantage of grassroots sport sponsorship includes increased availability for product sampling and prototype testing as additional ways to reach consumers. Greenwald and Fernandez-Balboa (1998) noted that, in grassroots sport sponsorship, "corporations are increasingly pumping money into grassroots sports organizations, and, in turn, grassroots sports organizations are better able to provide corporations with substantial returns on their investments" (p. 42). These companies are realizing that speaking to consumers in a local environment may be more persuasive than through nation-wide involvement.

One of the issues surrounding grassroots sport sponsorship is related to the professionalism of the local organization. This concern seems logical because national corporations tend to be less secure about putting their brand image in the hands of volunteers or unproven local organizers than they would be with major sport organizations or professional leagues. One industry executive commented, "There are just too many bad events. An event might have a couple of thousand kids, but not the media and PR. You pay a guy a couple of thousand dollars to support an event and you never know what happened" (Joyce, 2003, p. 8).

The quest for sponsors can be an exciting and rewarding one, but be assured that the sport marketer must consider the needs and objectives of the sponsor. The marketing director for Anaheim Sports cautioned sport administrators to avoid sponsor relationships that can evolve into situations in which the sponsors desire more for their money than has previously been delivered. He said, "We can't just put their sign up but must figure out how to drive traffic in their store or service" (Goldberg, 1998b). Sponsorship consultant Kim Skildum-Reid (2007) commented that "flashing your logo in front of masses of cynical consumers does not equal marketing return" (p. 4). The collective criteria used by sponsors to evaluate sponsorship opportunities do not seem to vary considerably from one company to another. However, each corporation, depending on its marketing strategy and current market position, values certain criteria differently. Therefore, sport marketers attempting to develop sponsorship proposals must understand the criteria and tailor proposals to specific sponsors.

BEST PRACTICE

FedEx's Sponsorship Recipe

With equal parts of local and national events with indirect revenue, FedEx has developed a portfolio framework that is integrated, actionable, and measurable and represents best practice in the field.

The portfolio is segmented by objective, not price. Internal teams are divided into two complementary camps, not one. And sponsorships as a tactical discipline are used in no less than five very different ways. Other brands focus on businesses [B–to–B] or consumers [B–to–C], but FedEx has to keep both on the radar screen. Although the primary target is in the B–to–B world, the company must build its umbrella name inside the B–to–B universe to ensure one of the most ubiquitous brands maintains its leadership status. "We are constantly reminding ourselves that we are not merely in the business of sponsoring things," said managing director of sponsorships Kevin Demsky. "We are in the business of convincing customers to utilize our services. Sponsorships are just a conduit to accomplishing the corporate objective."

That conduit plays a pivotal role inside the marketing machine, as evidenced by the business FedEx signs at events, the revenue generated direct from properties, and the strategic way the company uses sponsorships to invade new markets and maintain presence in existing operating regions. Using sponsorships, [FedEx] penetrated new areas and grew share faster than we could have before. They create an anchor point in the marketing mix.

FedEx has eight rules for winning the game of sponsorships:

1. Sponsorships Are Not Created Equal

There are five corporate goals for sponsorships: Drive revenue; provide an opportunity to entertain customers in a unique environment; give sales a platform for developing relationships; create benefits for employees; and drive the brand.

FedEx marketers realize few sponsorships can score five-for-five. "We recognize that not all properties can deliver on all goals," Demsky said. Different sponsorships deliver on different objectives and only when marketers acknowledge that can they develop a portfolio in which a series of properties achieve goals together. FedEx builds a "collection" of sponsorships that together helps move the needle.

2. Structure Portfolios by Objective, Not Price

If sponsorships are not created equal and can only achieve some of the five objectives, properties must be segmented into a portfolio that plays to the strengths and challenges of each. According to Demsky of FedEx, "Sponsorships deliver different benefits, so we've built a unique framework that allows us to see how our properties contribute." It's a strategic framework for defining the different pieces of the portfolio in a way that allows the company to analyze and make decisions on performance. FedEx uses a five-tier portfolio structure to categorize sponsorships by objective instead of by price (see below).

Category 5: Hospitality Events. Sponsorships should create "focused, private, extended" windows in which to invite customers to interact with FedEx. Such events are used to build relationships and learn more about prospects' businesses.

Category 4: Hometown Events. Through acquisition, FedEx's home is no longer solely in Memphis. For example, FedEx Ground is based in Pittsburgh, and FedEx Custom Critical operates in Akron, OH. Category 4 sponsorships keep the brand visible in the communities where it affects economic and social areas.

Category 3: Key Targets. This category was put in place to affect a specific geographic region or a specific demographic target. "For example, if our local marketing teams decide they need to penetrate Denver, my group will go out and set up a robust sponsorship plan to help drive business in that region," Demsky said.

Category 2: Revenue and Supply Chain Events. FedEx partners with properties that integrate the company's services into its own operations. The integration is then used as a compelling case study to share with customers and prospects about how FedEx helps businesses run more smoothly. Direct revenue is a secondary benefit for the property buying FedEx's services.

Category 1: Leadership Events. The crown jewels leveraged across multiple channels and used on a national basis achieve most of the five corporate goals. "We can do a little bit of everything with these events," Demsky said. "This is the one category that, because we can do so many things, we invest in a variety of activation vehicles."

In a system based on objectives, size doesn't matter. A FedEx Forum sits in Category 4, an NFL in Category 1, and FedEx Field, used to incorporate FedEx into the critical Washington, DC market, in Category 3. "The structure allows us to tailor our investments," said VP of marketing Brian Phillips. "Each property comes with a different set of expectations, and we calibrate our ROI calculation based on the category."

3. Measure Independently

An organization that treats every sponsorship independently needs an ROI system that measures each property singularly.

The company is getting ready to come out of the closet with an Index Measurement Tool that will calculate specific ratings based on property performance. "If we have a category model that recognizes no two sponsorships are the same, then we need a tool that will give us an accurate barometer to see if events are doing what we expect them to do," Demsky said.

The tool involves an "objective template" that is laid on top of sponsorships to generate a score that indicates whether or not an event is performing. The different scores are then combined to gauge the performance of the overall portfolio. "We don't expect a FedEx Field to have the same ROI as a PGA, so the Index Tool will help normalize the differences between properties and help us measure events on equal footing," Demsky said.

If a property scores poorly, FedEx will meet with the partner and try to identify ways to raise the number. If the score still remains low, it's an indication that the property may be ready for elimination from the portfolio.

4. Pass on Awareness

If a property primarily represents impressions, FedEx takes a pass—quickly. After all, with recognition near 100%, eyeballs are appreciated but not necessary.

"Certainly awareness is something that we are interested in creating, but only if it's a byproduct of a sponsorship," Demsky said. "In the hierarchy of benefits that come from sponsorship investments, it's not high on our list of must-haves."

More important are elements that push leads, anchor the brand, and provide face time. Impressions end up as icing on the sponsorship cake. "This company is measured by how many packages are shipped, and our sponsorships are measured by their contribution in driving those shipments," Demsky said. "It's too easy to get focused on how many eyeballs saw the brand that you lose focus on how many of those eyeballs pulled out their wallets."

5. Sponsorships 'Plus-Up' the Mix

Smart marketers integrate sponsorships throughout the marketing mix, not the other way around. "Certainly advertising, direct-response, and promotions are important on their own, but sponsorships provide a healthy way to plus-up the marketing mix beyond the events," said David Grant, a principal with longtime FedEx event agency Velocity Sports & Entertainment, Wilton, CT. "Sponsorship is a tool in and of itself, but it's also a tool to make everything else a little bit better. We're now using sponsorships as a more strategic tool and recognizing that we can integrate our events throughout the entire mix."

6. A House with Two Sides

Without a solid internal structure, sponsorships can't be identified, managed, or serviced. Keep it simple and focused by creating two sides to the sponsorship team, one that manages the present and another that focuses on the future. FedEx has a core team of 11 in-house members in its event department. One of the teams is focused on activating and leveraging investments already made via marketing programs, promotional components, hospitality efforts, and so on. On the other side of the house is another team responsible for managing the growth of the portfolio. They identify new sponsorship opportunities, decide whether or not the portfolio has the right mix, and oversee all selection, planning, and negotiations. Each team has staffers attached to specific properties. They manage all aspects of the deals, working with rights-holders, as well as other FedEx business units that may leverage the sponsorships.

7. Make Hospitality a Marketing Extension

Hospitality elements provide a platform for live extensions of branding. A sport organization's tagline, images, thematics, and attributes should come alive on-site. FedEx ties hospitality to different umbrella marketing messages. The Super Bowl annually sports hospitality interactives tied to the Air and Ground offerings. PGA events are used to showcase FedEx's reliability. At Gillette Stadium, the company brought its new "Relax. It's FedEx" tagline to life with a Relax Zone boasting soothing music, candles, and massages.

Hospitality must also be immersive. At the St. Jude Classic, for instance, FedEx erects a two-story structure that rivals any golf clubhouse. It's less about food and drinks and more about isolated environments for building relationships. "We've learned the average company employee doesn't have the authority to choose which company their employer uses to ship a package," Demsky said. "And for those individuals that do have the authority, it's a complicated decision. So in order to help our salespeople get some time with those customers, we create the quality time in which to have a discussion."

FedEx also makes the most of hospitality with off-hour events for customers and prospects. For example, last winter the company created NFL Open Houses in five markets in which as many as 500 customers were brought in on an off-day for activities, entertainment, behind-the-scenes tours, and chalk talks with players. The hospitality blueprint follows no less than Six Points of Communication with the target called pre-invite, formal "save the date" invitation, a "what to expect" message, itinerary, the on-site event, and a follow-up.

8. Say When

There's nothing wrong with window-shopping, but event marketers should know when the portfolio has had enough. "If you have 20 properties that you need to actively leverage, you have too many properties," Grant said. If the return is not meeting objectives, then it may be more of an issue in which property is not delivering rather than one in which property needs to be added.

Cover Story: Game On. (2004, May 4). *Event Marketer*. Retrieved June 22, 2004, from http://www.eventmarketer.com/viewMedia.asp?prmMID=511

Reprinted with permission.

Recommended Additional Reading

Motion, J., Leitch, S., & Brodie, R. (2003). Equity in corporate co-branding. *European Journal of Marketing, 37*(7/8), 1080–1094.

Sponsor Needs Worksheets

The worksheets provide a guide for developing various sections of your sponsorship plan. The following sheets cover sponsor needs and rationale. Complete this worksheet as you would prepare a sponsorship plan.

Identify the demographics of your team event and match them to those of your potential sponsor.

_____

_____

_____

_____

_____

_____

_____

_____

Determine the psychographic and image match between the sponsor's product and your property.

_____

_____

_____

_____

_____

Enumerate possible awareness objectives that could be accomplished through the sponsorship.

_____

_____

_____

_____

Cite possible image objectives that could be accomplished through the sponsorship.

_____

_____

_____

_____

_____

_____

Itemize possible sales objectives that could be accomplished through the sponsorship.

_____

_____

_____

_____

_____

Describe possible hospitality objectives that could be accomplished through the sponsorship.

_____

_____

_____

_____

_____

Present possible employee motivation objectives that could be accomplished through the sponsorship.

_____

_____

_____

_____

_____

_____

_____

Determine and describe the potential for on-site sales and wholesaler tie-ins that could be accomplished through the sponsorship.

_____

_____

_____

_____

_____

Discuss the potential for cross-promotions that could be possible through the sponsorship.

_____

_____

_____

_____

_____

_____

Consider potential issues in integrated communications regarding the timing of the sponsorship and the sponsor's business activities.

_____
_____
_____
_____
_____

List all current sponsors and reflect on any conflicts that may surface.

_____
_____
_____
_____
_____

Detail the nature of cooperation obtained from the venue/facility.

_____
_____
_____
_____
_____

Outline any conceivable risks that may result from the sponsorship.

_____
_____
_____
_____
_____

Discuss the potential of all cause-related sponsorship options.

_____
_____
_____
_____
_____

Determine if any grassroots sponsorship options may be available for sponsors.

_____
_____
_____
_____
_____

Chapter Four

OLYMPIC SPONSORSHIP OPPORTUNITIES

The Olympic Movement and Sponsorship

Olympic and amateur sport organizations, throughout the past Olympiads, have become increasingly dependent upon corporate sponsors who have supplied much-needed revenue in difficult financial times. The dependency of the Olympic movement on corporate sponsors is evidenced by the statistic showing that just over 30% of the International Olympic Committee's budget, and about 40% of the United States Olympic Committee's (USOC) funds, are derived from sponsorship and licensing income (Olympic Fact File, 2000). Specifically, for the period ending in 2002, the USOC had revenues totaling $129,521,000 with income from its joint sponsorship program at $29.6 million and royalty and rights fees totaling $10.2 million and $22.1 million respectively (United States Olympic Committee, 2002). Olympic organizing committees are also increasingly dependent on these resources. Sponsorship revenue for the 2002 Olympic Games accounted for 54% of all income. These sources accounted for 43% of the budget used to produce the Nagano Winter Olympic Games and were somewhat less than the budget for Sydney, which was 34% (Olympic Fact File, 1998, 2000, 2008; International Olympic Committee, 2004b). Projections for the 2010 Winter Olympic Games showed that 42% of the Vancouver Organizing Committee (VANOC) revenues were derived from sponsorships (Hotzau, 2007a).

One aspect of the Olympic movement that has attracted sponsors is the global power represented in the Olympic symbol, the five interlocking rings. The Olympic rings have shown to be the most recognizable logo in the world with 89.8% of the population capable of correctly recognizing the symbol (TOP IV Programme, 1997). Thus, associating with the Olympic rings would be highly prized by leading corporations, and it could increase corporate exposure to the cumulative worldwide television audience of 4 billion viewers who typically watch the Games either in-person or through the global television coverage (Olympic Fact File, 2004).

Sponsorship and the Olympic Games have existed since the Games' inception. In ancient Greece, City-States and merchants supported many athletes. With the revival of the Games in 1896, Kodak placed an ad in the official program of the first modern Olympics. It was in 1928 that Coca-Cola began its long-standing relationship with the Olympic movement (Pratzmark & Frey, 1989). Sponsorship and the Olympics have a well-established relationship and one that has significantly increased in complexity.

Commercialization of the Olympic Games

Sport industry witnessed a transition between the 1976 Montreal Olympic Games and the 1984 Los Angeles Games. Currently, most people are aware of the intense financial burden, of a more than $1 billion debt that the 1976 Games placed on Montreal, and the overt commercialization of the 1984 Games, as well. Through its efforts in attracting corporate sponsors, the Los Angeles Olympic Organizing Committee was able to operate the Games and generate a profit in excess of $225 million. "There [were] plenty of opportunities for sale in the five-ring circus: television, commercials, product licensing, product exclusivity at the Games, team sponsorships, Olympic movement sponsorships, awards presentations, training center support, product endorsements, and almost anything a marketing [person] could devise" (Marsano, 1987, p. 65). Since the commercialization in 1984 and the realization of substantial profits, sponsorship has become an integral part of the Olympic movement.

Corporate rationale for Olympic sponsorship is quite similar to the rationale for other sponsorship activities. Carter and Wilkinson (2002) explored sponsor rationale for the 2000 Sydney Games. They found that the top ranked objective was increasing brand awareness, followed by reaching an appropriate audience, showcasing products, and increasing employee morale. Results from their study showed that hospitality objectives were ranked somewhat lower than in other studies. It is important to note that there was significant variance between these factors and the level of sponsorship which demonstrated that different sponsors sought different objectives. Furthermore, Carter and Wilkinson's research (2002) indicates that high levels variance also exist between sponsoring companies.

Olympic Sponsorship Rights and Privileges

There are five different types of Olympic sponsorships in which corporations could become involved: national governing bodies, national olympic committees, Olympic organizing committees, the IOC's worldwide Olympic sponsorship program, and the International Olympic Committee itself. Each entity provides specific sponsor rights associated with participation.

NATIONAL GOVERNING BODIES

At the base of the Olympic organization, the national governing bodies (NGBs) have engaged in a variety of sponsorship activities. Each Olympic sport has an NGB in each country that is a member of the IOC. These organizations can grant sponsorship rights to companies for activities for their sport within a single country. It is important to understand that sponsors of NGBs can gain access to the team members of that sport, the uniforms of that sport, and the NGB's logo but not the Olympic rings. U.S. Ski Team has successfully managed its sponsorship programs for many years independently from the USOC. In 2007, they signed a sponsorship agreement with Audi as Official Automotive Sponsor of the U.S. Ski Team. Audi's chief marketing officer commented that "the US ski team is a globally recognized symbol of peak performance and precision, making it a perfect fit with Audi's Quattro all wheel drive system and Audi's world-renowned luxury vehicles" (Audi of America, 2007, ¶3).

USA Gymnastics continues to work with Olympic sponsor VISA. The two signed an agreement for VISA to be the title sponsor of the USA Gymnastics Championships, to be called the VISA Championships, from 2005 to 2008. Through the sponsorship, VISA also becomes the official payment sponsor. USA Gymnastics President Bob Colarossi said, "VISA has been a valuable contributor and marketing partner for the organization and we look forward to another successful Olympic quadrennium together as we jointly develop programs for the 2008 Beijing Olympic Games" (Eaton, 2004, p. 9).

The U.S. Soccer Federation recently signed Nike to a 10-year sponsorship worth $120 million. Their agreement stipulates that Nike will support youth development programs and provide equipment and uniforms to all US national teams. Nike also secured deals with soccer governing bodies in several other nations, including some of the world's top teams, the Netherlands, Brazil, Nigeria, and South Korea. Miller Brewing Company also teamed up with a national governing body when it signed up as a sponsor for the Mexican National Soccer Team to promote its brands in Mexico.

Several successful national governing body (NGB) sponsorship arrangements were consummated for the Athens Olympic Games. Nautica International signed up as the official apparel supplier for US Sailing, and through the arrangement, Nautica supplied outfits for the 130 members of the US Sailing Team, the US Disabled Sailing Team, and the US Sailing World Youth Team ("Nautica signs," 2004).

Another NGB, USA Team Handball, created a rather unique sponsorship opportunity: Team Handball created an innovative program where individual citizens and schools could "adopt" a USA Team Handball team member for the Olympic Games. "Adoption papers" cost only $35.00 per athlete and brought much-needed funding to USA Team Handball. In addition, it generated a significant amount of publicity and created excitement about the sport in numerous communities across the country.

NATIONAL OLYMPIC COMMITTEES

A national Olympic committee (NOC) can authorize the use of the Olympic rings but only in conjunction with its respective logo. For the United States Olympic Committee (USOC), that would mean using the designated symbols of the USOC as defined in its graphic standards manual. The most frequently used USOC symbol depicts the Olympic rings accompanied by the letters USA. Any USOC logo must, of course, adhere to the rigorous specifications outlined by the USOC. For the quadrennium ending in 2008, the USOC secured sponsorships at the "Partner" level, the highest level offered by the USOC, with AT&T, Anheuser-Busch, General Motors, Bank of America, and ChevronTexaco. All domestic partners, sponsors, and suppliers receive marketing rights to the US Olympic Team and commercial access to Olympic themes, terminology, and imagery for use in sponsor marketing and advertising programs. These sponsors would have the right to proclaim themselves as USOC sponsors and sponsors of the US Olympic Team. For example, Nike secured the rights through 2012 as the Official Outfitter of the US Olympic Team "allowing," or requiring, athletes to showcase Nike products on the medals podium at the Olympic Games. Clothier Ralph Lauren signed in 2008 as the provider of apparel for the opening and closing ceremonies of the Beijing Olympic Games.

According to the USOC, "the 'Sponsor' level represents the level of corporate support required to gain access to the USA-5 ring logo as an 'Official Sponsor' and commercial access to Olympic themes, terminology, and imagery for use in sponsor marketing programs." "USOC Sponsors" provide significant levels of cash, products, or services in support of the US Olympic Team and may also choose to extend their US Olympic investment to include National NGBs, the US Paralympic Team, and/or US Olympic Signature Property events and programs. Sponsors at this level include such companies as Allstate Insurance, Kellogg, Home Depot, Hallmark, Office Depot, PowerBar, United Airlines, and 24 Hour Fitness, among others. PowerBar supplied more than 600,000 energy bars to the US Olympic Team over the past few years, as the "Official Nutritional Energy Bar Supplier" for the US Olympic Team. An array of other companies has bought in at the "Supplier" level that provides access only to the USOC supplier logo that also includes the rings. "All domestic partners, sponsors, and suppliers receive marketing rights to the US Olympic Team and conduct all advertising and marketing programs within the US" (United States Olympic Committee, 2004, p. 37).

Motivations driving the USOC sponsorship vary. Bank of America's chief marketing officer commented, "The Olympic Games are watched by a broad and diverse audience of Americans, and we expect the 2008 Olympic Games in Beijing will draw record television ratings in the United States and worldwide. As the nation's largest consumer bank, and one with corporate clients in more than 150 countries, the Olympic Games enable our brand to reach hundreds of millions of consumers and corporate customers" (Bank of America, 2004). Value-in-kind was a great benefit of the USOC's arrangement with ChevronTexaco during the 2004 Athens Olympic Games. The USOC had budgeted over $1 million for accommodations for its officials yet was able to secure a cruise ship from Royal Olympic by trading fuel received as part of its sponsorship with ChevronTexaco (Woodward, 2004).

Because the 2002 Olympic Games were held in the United States (Salt Lake City), the USOC developed a new marketing and sponsorship program in 1998 entitled Olympic Properties of the United States (OPUS). This program was designed with constructs similar to those of the ACOP program administered for the 1996 Atlanta Games. This program provided access to the benefits offered by the USOC together with properties associated with the Salt Lake Organizing Committee. One of the new sponsors signed up by OPUS was General Motors. The $1 billion, eight-year deal allowed GM to market a variety of vehicles to the diverse audience that the Olympic Games represented and to introduce new models in conjunction with the launch of each Olympic Games during the contract period (Rozin, 1998).

Interestingly, Olympic training centers around the U.S. are responsible for securing their own sponsorship arrangements. However, in most cases, they work very closely with the USOC marketing and sponsorship division. Many of the Olympic Training Center agreements encompass in-kind donations of products and services.

OLYMPIC ORGANIZING COMMITTEES

The Olympic organizing committees (OOCs) have also benefited from both television revenues and from sponsorship agreements. Worldwide television revenues for the 2008 Beijing Olympic Games were estimated at $1.7 billion (yes, billion). In 2004, the formula for allocation of Olympic television rights changed such that the funds would be shared on the basis of 49% to the OOC and 51% to the Olympic movement. The specific breakout specifies that the IOC share revenues with the International Federations (IFs) for the Summer and Winter sports. In 2006, the Winter IFs received $126 million, and in 2004, the Summer Games IFs got $254 million. A review of the TV rights fees paid by U.S. broadcasting companies has been provided at the conclusion of this chapter. As noted earlier, as much as 50% of an organizing committee's budget may be generated through sponsorships. The rights involved with an organizing committee may include official suppliers, sponsors, and licensing agreements. The 2004 Athens Games brought in $776 million from its partnerships, while Salt Lake City brought in $876 million (Olympic Fact File, 2008).

The organizing committee is able to reduce budget demands through the value-in-kind (VIK) supplies, and the sponsor is able to associate its products/services with the Games. Some of the more traditional examples include the sponsorship of awards, transportation, communication systems, and various sport-specific equipment. In 2008, Beijing was able to secure sponsorship from China Mobile for cell phone service, SinoPec for fuel, and Volkswagen for official vehicles. Interestingly, Volkswagen paid $100 million for these rights while adidas paid $80 million, both higher than fees paid by the IOC's Worldwide Olympic sponsors. It seems that access to 1.3 billion people has value. In total, the Beijing Organizing Committee (BOCOG) generated $750 million in sponsorship revenues through 11 "Games Partners," 10 "Exclusive Suppliers," and 15 "Official Suppliers" (http://en.beijing 2008.cn/bocog/sponsors/sponsors). Ventures such as these have been very popular with both organizing committees and sponsors.

THE OLYMPIC PARTNERS

In 1985, the IOC created a program to make the world's most complicated sport marketing purchase a "one-stop shopping" venture for international corporations (Marsano, 1987, p. 65). No longer would companies endure the trauma of multiple negotiations that often produced only narrow results. What ensued was known as "The Olympic Programme," now entitled The Olympic Partners (TOP). The first TOP program covered 1985 to 1988, while TOP II provided sponsors with benefits from 1989 to 1992 and TOP III regulated sponsor activity from 1990 to 1996. Similarly, TOP IV's time frame included the 1998 Nagano Olympic and the 2000 Olympic Games in Sydney. TOP V covered the Winter Games of 2002 in Salt

Lake City and the 2004 Summer Games in Athens, while the TOP VI program included Torino and Beijing (Olympic Fact File, 2008).

The system was patterned after the success of the Los Angeles Games, which demonstrated that having fewer sponsors who paid more money was better for organizers and sponsors alike. TOP established a system whereby a limited number of sponsors would receive special treatment and benefits on a worldwide basis while achieving product category exclusivity and protection for their Olympic sponsorship activities. Specifically, TOP Sponsors receive the following benefits (International Olympic Committee, 2004):

1. Product Exclusivity—Only one sponsor is allowed for any product category. This means that as long as Coca-Cola and VISA are members of the TOP, Pepsi and American Express will not be allowed to become involved with Olympic sponsorship on any level, international, national, or with the organizing committee.

2. Use of Olympic Marks, Imagery, and Designations—Each participant is granted the right to use the solitary Olympic rings, as well as, use of the rings in combination with all 202 NOC designations. This provides both worldwide and local impact. Companies can also use the "Official Sponsor" and "Official Product" designations for all organizing committees in addition to the OOC logos.

3. Public Relations and Promotional Opportunities—Sponsors are given special tie-ins and media events to increase their exposure.

4. Access to Olympic Archives—The IOC makes available articles, photographs, and video footage from the Olympic museum and archives in Switzerland to sponsors for special exhibits and displays.

5. Olympic Merchandise and Premiums—Clothing and apparel bearing the Olympic logos can be used for sales incentives and marketing activities organized by each sponsor.

6. Tickets and Hospitality—Sponsors receive priority access to seating at both the Winter and Summer Games.

7. Advertising Options—Each participant in TOP is given first chance at souvenir program ads and the "right of first refusal" in purchasing advertising on Olympic broadcasts.

8. On-Site Participation—Point-of-purchase and product display are included in the package. Companies gain certain rights to concession areas and space for product sampling. Showcase opportunities are also made available on the Olympic venue grounds.

9. Research—Each sponsor receives a full research report on the public's reception of the company's participation and an assessment of the value-added benefits.

10. First Right of Negotiation for the Next Quadrennial—All worldwide sponsors with TOP have the option to continue in their product category.

The nine initial clients in the TOP I program contributed a total of $95 million in revenues. For sponsors, TOP I proved to be a resounding success in 1988. Subsequently, the program produced $175 million for TOP II, $350 for TOP III, and $500 million for TOP IV, ending with the Sydney Games (TOP IV Programme, 1997). The TOP V program, which covered the 2002 Winter Games in Salt Lake

City and the 2004 Summer Games in Athens, generated $663 million, while the TOP VI program of Torino and Beijing generated $866 million in revenues (Olympic Fact File, 2008).

TOP VII companies and their representative categories, through the London and Vancouver Olympic Games, were not finalized as of the publication of this text. However, TOP VI members included (International Olympic Committee, 2008):

Company	Category
Coca-Cola	Nonalcoholic beverage
Atos Origin	Information technology
Manulife	Life insurance/Annuities
Kodak	Film/Photography and imaging (not renewing after 2008)
VISA	Consumer payment systems
Panasonic-Matsushita	Television/Video/Audio Equipment
Samsung	Wireless communications equipment
McDonald's	Retail food services
General Electric	Various equipment and services
Omega	Timing, scoring, and venue Results
Lenovo	Computing technology (not renewing after 2008, replaced by Acer)

Kodak was actually an advertiser in the program for the first Olympics of the modern era in 1896, and Coca-Cola became a supplier for the Olympics in 1928. Many of the others joined in 1988 when the TOP program was initiated, while Samsung and McDonald's signed-up as members of the TOP IV program in 1997. The arrangement with Samsung provided the 1998 and 2000 Games with wireless communications equipment. This asset was deemed to be "vital to the achievement of a smooth and successful running of the Games" (Two New Partners, 1997, p. 9). In addition, they provided over 20,000 cellular telephones to officials and participating teams. Another unique service was their "call home" program which allowed athletes to contact their families immediately after their events (Worldwide TOP Programme, 1998). Samsung's Group President remarked, "The Olympic spirit of world peace and contribution to society is at one with Samsung's ideals (Olympic Fact File, 1998, p. 54). McDonald's decided to expand its 1996 sponsorship activities in Atlanta's Olympic Village, and through the past years has become a worldwide partner by activating its sponsorship, not only at the Games, but in its restaurants in the 202 countries involved in the Games. In 2008 for the Beijing Olympics, the McDonald's Olympic Champion Crew program recognized and rewarded 1,400 of its best-of-the-best restaurant employees from around the world with travel to Beijing to serve the world's best athletes and thousands of others at McDonald's four new Olympic venue restaurants.

For McDonald's, the rationale was customer oriented: "Now all of our customers around the world can share in the fun and excitement of the Olympic Games" (Olympic Fact File, 1998, p. 53). McDonald's leveraged its "Worldwide Partner" status with the Canadian Olympic Committee by supporting Olympic School Day runs across Canada prior to the Games. Other global activities included a European program called "Go Active" featuring the promotion of adult happy meals that included a salad, water, and free stepometer. In China, they featured cups with Olympic athletes, and in Japan, they ran an Olympic-themed game with instant-win coupons and premium prizes. Swatch joined in 2003 and Lenovo joined in 2004 for the 2006 to 2008 quadrennium. Lenovo, feeling as those it had accomplished its objectives, dropped out after the 2008 Games.

The disbursement policy provides that revenues derived from the TOP program must be shared. The proportion of revenues allocated to the various Olympic entities is as follows (Greater TOP support, 1997; Michel, 1991; International Olympic Committee, 2008):

- 40% of the funds are allotted to the participating national Olympic committees. The precise distribution is based on a formula whereby the money is divided with each NOC* receiving a set dollar amount (minimum of $40,000) plus an additional amount per athlete qualifying for the Games.

- Since TOP's inception 20 years ago, the USOC has received 20% of all TOP funds. The original leverage was based on the high proportion of sponsors and broadcast monies originating from US companies. US sources currently account for 62% of revenues. In 2008, many IOC members were calling for a revision of this revenue sharing formula.

- 50% of the funds are disbursed to the participating Olympic organizing committees. Within these parameters, the Winter Games Organizing Committee receives 10% of the monies while the Summer Games Organizing Committee is allotted 40%.

- The IOC keeps the remaining 10%.

The corporations involved in TOP have a significant involvement in the Games and present a myriad of justifications and explanations for their participation (12 Top Companies, 1991; Worldwide TOP Programme, 1998; Olympic Fact File, 1998 & 2008; International Olympic Committee, 2002b).

The Olympic Games present a variety of opportunities for Coke. They continue to sponsor the Olympic Torch Relay and the popular on-site Olympic Pin Trading Centre. To promote its products, Coke supplies the Olympic village with "no charge" vending machines and has exclusive pouring rights for beverages at Olympic venues. Coke's Board of Directors Chair said, "As a global company, we feel it is important for us to be a part of such a powerful movement" ("Olympic Fact File," 1998, p. 51).

Kodak has been part of the Olympic movement from the beginning of the modern Games. Kodak products were advertised in the book of official results for the first Olympiad of the modern era—Athens, 1896. Kodak's Olympic tradition continues with multiple goals. Those goals are, in simplest terms, building a positive image for Kodak, its products, and its employees; promoting the highest ideals of sportsmanship; and fostering friendly competition among nations. "Kodak is in the business of capturing and sharing moments, and few events create positive memories quite like the Olympic Games" (Kodak and the Games, 2004). In support of these goals, Kodak operated the world's largest photo lab at the 2004 Athens Games providing digital and film processing for professional photographers and spectators alike. Accredited photographers used the 18,000 square foot main media center, and Kodak Picturemaker kiosks were located around the venues to assist spectators with their photographic needs and allowing them to "instantly share their digital photos with friends and family around the world" (Kodak and the Games, 2004, ¶2). In addition, Kodak teamed with another sponsor, Atos-Origin, to produce the 350,000 accreditation badges needed for the Games.

Olympic sponsorship has been of immense benefit to the VISA brand and overall image. As noted in Chapter 9, VISA has gained substantial market share through its Olympic involvement and has been very successful through advertising, which highlights its exclusive vendor position with Olympic ticket sales. As a part of its TOP program, it has established special VISA NET systems to link thousands of ATMs in over 200 countries. It has also supported a variety of the cultural and educational exhibits during the Games. The benefit of Olympic sponsorship for VISA was activating a "powerful tool to help us achieve our objectives of building the VISA brand and providing our members and merchants with opportunities to build their business. No single sponsorship property has delivered stronger returns for our members and merchants than the Olympic Games" (VISA USA, 2004, p. 2).

The Olympic Games provide an opportunity for Panasonic to showcase its technology as the principal contractor for the International Broadcast Centre (IBC). The IBC is the facility from which all television signals emanate. In addition to the IBC, Panasonic provides more than 20 giant screens and video-on-demand units at various locations in the Olympic host city. The rationale provided by Panasonic's president centered on having its corporate name "associated with this premier international athletic event" (Olympic Fact File, 1998, p. 53). Furthermore, General Electric has used its sponsorship to demonstrate its technological capabilities across a variety of industries, from broadcast (e.g., NBC) to medical technology (e.g., MRI) used in the Olympic medical centers.

TOP has served two major goals of the Olympic movement. It has made the IOC less dependent on television revenues, and it has assisted all countries in the world with sport development through a shared revenue system.

Paralympics

Another Olympic-related event is the Paralympic Games. The Summer and Winter events follow the regularly scheduled Olympic Games by two weeks and provide competition for the world's elite disabled athletes. This differs appreciably from the Special Olympics, which provide opportunities for mentally disabled participants. The Paralympics have been extremely successful in showcasing the talents of elite athletes with disabilities, such as blindness, amputation, or paralysis. "The first Paralympics were held in 1960 in Rome, Italy. Only 400 athletes from 23 countries participated. It wasn't until the 1988 Paralympics in Seoul, Korea that the modern-day practice of the Olympic-host nation also hosted the Paralympic Games. Today more than 4,000 athletes from 120 countries participate in the Summer Paralympics, while more than 1,100 athletes from 36 countries compete in the Winter

Paralympic Games" (http://paralympics.teamusa.org). The U.S. Paralympic team's mission is "to be the world leader in the Paralympic movement by developing comprehensive and sustainable elite programs integrated into Olympic National Governing Bodies. To utilize our Olympic and Paralympic platform to promote excellence in the lives of persons with disabilities" (http://paralympics.teamusa.org).

As an affiliate of the USOC, ties with USOC sponsors are strong; however, the U.S. Paralympic organization has the right to pursue sponsorship independently. In 2004, just prior to the Athens Olympics, the U.S. Paralympic team secured a sponsorship from DaimlerChrysler Vans as its official vehicle sponsor. Daimler-Chrysler is working with Olympic gold medalist Chris Waddell to reach out to rehabilitation hospitals across the U.S. through a multiple city tour. Although General Motors is an official sponsor of the USOC, they did not have the funds to support the U.S. Paralympic team for Athens. In conversations with GM, former U.S. Paralympic executive director Charlie Hubner was granted permission to seek support from DaimlerChrysler for 2004. GM agreed to support the Paralympic team through the 2008 Beijing Games. Similarly, TOP sponsor John Hancock allowed U.S. Paralympics to pursue and secure The Hartford as its insurance sponsor, based in part on The Hartford's long time association with disabled sport.

Both Bank of America and Nike, who sponsor the USOC, also contribute to the U.S. Paralympic team. The division of funds between the USOC and Paralympics in handled internally, but the support is significant to the U.S. Paralympic team's success. The USOC provides other funding for the U.S. Paralympic team, but the funding provided for Paralympic athletes is substantially less than that provided for the able-bodied Olympic athletes and increases the need of the organization to seek sponsors independently.

Ambush Marketing

As the cost of obtaining sponsorship rights with sport organizations began to escalate, some companies started to explore methods that could deliver the same impact as a sport sponsorship but at a reduced cost. Some corporate marketers decided they would attempt to associate their company with sport events without paying the requisite sponsorship fee. This tactic soon became known as "ambush marketing." Ambush marketing has been defined as "a promotional strategy whereby a non-sponsor attempts to capitalize on the popularity/prestige of a property by giving the false impression that it is a sponsor. [This tactic is] often employed by the competitors of a property's official sponsors" (Ukman, 1995, p. 42). Several prominent examples of ambush marketing have developed within the sport industry, and it appears that the practice is still growing (Hotzau, 2007b).

Significant debate surrounds the practice of ambush marketing. Skildum-Reid noted that everyone has an opinion. "It's stealing, it's cleaver, it's guerrilla marketing; when it happens, the topic always turns to ethics. Is it right or is it wrong?" (Skildum-Reid, 2007, p. xii).

The recent history of ambush marketing started at the 1984 Olympic Games when Kodak cleverly ambushed Fuji Film. Although Fuji had purchased the right to be an official sponsor from the Los Angeles Olympic Organizing Committee, the public was convinced that Kodak, not Fuji, was the official sponsor (Hotzau, 2007b). By purchasing sponsorships with the USOC and buying numerous television ads during the Games, Kodak created the perception that they were an official sponsor of the Olympic Games. Kodak did not mislead the public but merely leveraged the public's ignorance about the recently conceived Olympic sponsorship concept.

In some instances, the Olympic organizers are partially to blame for allowing ambush marketing activities. In an effort to commemorate the Games, the Los Angeles City Council approved a name-change for one of its thoroughfares to "Olympic Boulevard." As a result, hundreds of businesses relocated to the street and opened up with names like Olympic Cleaners and Olympic Limousines. These measures were deemed to be legal because businesses were allowed, under city statute, to use their street location name as part of their business identity.

Nike cleverly had murals painted on the sides of assorted downtown Los Angeles buildings during the 1984 Games (Myerson, 1996). The same strategy was averted for 1996 in Atlanta when the City Council passed a ban on large-scale outdoor advertising. Reebok officials unsuccessfully argued that its proposed 60-by-80-foot mural of Shaquille O'Neal was public art. However, several companies discovered a loophole because the regulations did not include large portable signage or building-sized projected images (Bayor, 1996).

American Express and VISA have had continuous battles over legitimate sponsorship rights and alleged ambush tactics since 1988. VISA aired advertising that claimed that the Olympics would not take American Express cards. This was technically accurate in reference to the official ticket outlets. However, various tour companies and other travel-related services would accept American Express cards in payment. During the 1992 Barcelona Games, American Express constructed its own advertising campaign claiming that you did not need a Visa, as opposed to VISA card, to go to Barcelona (Hotzau, 2007b). Note that no mention was made of the Olympic Games. As a final ploy in its strategy, American Express purchased sponsorship rights to the hotel key fobs at the IOC headquarters hotel in Barcelona. The key fobs were shaped and colored like an American Express card on one side and had hotel information on the other.

Ambush marketing tactics are not confined to overzealous corporations. The City of Atlanta Convention and Visitors Bureau tried to sell sponsorships during the 1996 Games in conflict with the Atlanta Olympic Organizing Committee program. They were, however, bought-off by the organizing committee for $3 million (Hotzau, 2007b). Former IOC Vice President Dick Pound commented, "It never occurred to anybody that a city would ever think of ambushing its own organizing committee" (Wells, 1996, p. 53). The IOC was so concerned about some citizens believing ambush marketing was clever or inspired that they began using the term "Parasite Marketing" to convey a less-than-positive impression of the practice. Protection against this type of ambush is now required in the bid documents submitted for consideration in hosting the Games. Beijing enacted the Olympic Signs Protection Act that came into effect on April 1, 2002 (Chua, 2002). Any infringement of the rules would first be dealt with through an order for cessation followed by confiscation and destruction of goods. Furthermore, the offender was required to forfeit all profits and could be fined up to five times the estimated profits (Chua, 2002). Similarly, the Italian government passed legislation in August 2005, specifically called Regulation #167, for the 2006 Winter Games, and Canada Passed the Olympic and Paralympic Marks Act for the 2010 Vancouver Games (Hotzau, 2007).

There is some concern that the IOC is not practicing what it preaches. In 1994, the IOC developed its own program for IOC sponsors, as opposed to Worldwide Olympic sponsors. The IOC sold an automobile sponsorship to Mercedes-Benz and a clothing deal to Mizuno, among others (Olympic Fact File, 2008). According to one industry leader, "We always thought it a bit underhanded that the International Olympic Committee had its own sponsors" (Ukman, 1998, p. 2).

The IOC, USOC, NGBs, sponsors, and broadcast networks have worked diligently to curtail ambush marketing of the Olympic Games. In 1996, the Atlanta Organizing Committee, together with the IOC, established a fund to publicize the names of ambush marketers in national newspapers. The advertising copy stated that "Deceptive advertising is not an Olympic sport" and "Every time a company runs an ad like this, our Olympic team loses" (Myerson, 1996, p. D1). These funds were not used and the threat seems to have had the desired results. Currently, the IOC requires the bid cities to enact legislation to control the illegal use of IOC and OOC marks. The IOC reported that, since 1996, the Olympics have been relatively free from ambush marketing activities.

Table 4.1. U.S. Television Rights Fees for the Olympic Games

Year	Site	Network	Price
1960	Squaw Valley (Winter)	CBS	$394,000
1960	Rome (Summer)	CBS	$550,000
1964	Innsbruck (Winter)	ABC	$597,000
1964	Tokyo (Summer)	NBC	$1.5 million
1968	Grenoble (Winter)	ABC	$2.5 million
1968	Mexico City (Summer)	ABC	$4.5 million
1972	Sapporo (Winter)	NBC	$6.4 million
1972	Munich (Summer)	ABC	$7.5 million
1976	Innsbruck (Winter)	ABC	$10 million
1976	Montreal (Summer)	ABC	$25 million
1980	Lake Placid (Winter)	ABC	$15.5 million
1980	Moscow (Summer)	NBC	$87 million
1984	Sarajevo (Winter)	ABC	$91.5 million
1984	Los Angeles (Summer)	ABC	$225 million
1988	Calgary (Winter)	ABC	$309 million
1988	Seoul (Summer)	NBC	$300 million
1992	Albertville (Winter)	CBS	$243 million
1992	Barcelona (Summer)	NBC	$401 million
1994	Lillehammer (Winter)	CBS	$300 million
1996	Atlanta (Summer)	NBC	$456 million
1998	Nagano (Winter)	CBS	$375 million
2000	Sydney (Summer)	NBC	$705 Million
2002	Salt Lake City (Winter)	NBC	$545 Million
2004	Athens (Summer)	NBC	$793 Million
2006	Turin (Winter)	NBC	$613 Million
2008	Beijing (Summer)	NBC	$894 Million
2010	Vancouver (Winter)	NBC	$820 Million
2012	London (Summer)	NBC	$1.18 Billion
2014	Sochi (Winter)	TBD	

Chapter Five

INDIVIDUAL ATHLETE SPONSORSHIPS

Introduction

In "ancient" times, like the 1960s, few athletes were able to obtain individual sponsorship deals. There were salaries for professional players and prize money for tournament winners, yet endorsements were few and far between. Big name players in golf, like Arnold Palmer, Gary Player, and Jack Nicklaus, or tennis stars, such as Billie Jean King and Stan Smith, accorded attention and secured sponsorship deals. However, in 1972, a young, attractive swimmer (who shall remain nameless) won seven gold medals in the Olympics and proceeded to price himself out of the business. This marked a turbulent time in the individual endorsement arena. However, the 1980s marked a revolution in athlete endorsements. The shoe and equipment companies literally fought over the top players, and endorsement fees escalated through the mid-90s. However, when a recession hit the shoe industry in the later part of the decade, many companies reduced the number of athletes receiving large endorsement fees. The result was that, while fewer players actually received contracts, the size of the contract for each athlete increased. The market rebounded in the early 2000s, and all of the leading manufacturers expanded their existing and long-term commitments for player endorsements.

Brooks and Harris (1998) provided a conceptual framework through which sport marketers could examine athletic endorsements. They set forward four classifications of endorsement protocol. The first category was "(a) the explicit mode ('I endorse this product'), (b) the implicit mode ('I use this product'), (c) the imperative mode ('You should use this product'), and (d) the co-present mode (the athlete merely appears in some setting with the product)" (Brooks & Harris, 1998, p. 36). Stone, Joseph, and Jones (2003) forwarded several factors that corporations should evaluate before selecting athletes for endorsements. They suggest that the athlete should be high in trustworthiness, be easily recognizable by the target audience, be affordable for the sponsor, be of little risk for negative publicity, and be well matched with the product. Substantial research has also shown how the fit between an athlete and the products that he or she endorses is critical factor. Following are several examples to illustrate these points.

The lure of sport personalities has been present for decades. Just as Arnold Palmer and Michael Jordan spoke to their generations, action sport athletes Shaun White and Leanne Pelosi speak to another. Shaun's sponsors include Burton snowboards, Oakley, Birdhouse Skateboards, Park City Resort, Red Bull, Target stores, Adio, and Hewlett-Packard. Pelosi's sponsors include ThirtyTwo, etnies Girl, K2, Dragon, Bonfire, Dakine, Red Bull, Vestal, Solo Mobile, Whistler/Blackcomb, and Coastal Riders Snowboard Shop. Blazing the trail for other action sport athletes, Dave Mira and Tony Hawk were among the first to have contracts and endorsements with shoe companies and sport clothiers, as well as their own video games—BMX and Pro Skater, respectively (Bennett, Henson, & Zhang, 2002; Goldman, 2000). Hawk secured endorsement contracts estimated at $10 million per year, and his video game has been one of the top selling sports video games in the history of the industry.

Michael Jordan defined sport endorsements when he was with the National Basketball Association's (NBA) Chicago Bulls. He serves as the classic example of the way in which a player can build capital through salaries and sponsorship agreements. With a $28 million contract for his playing ability, Jordan could have probably survived, to say the least. But when his contracts from outside endorsements and sponsorships were included, he might even have been considered wealthy. Jordan signed an endorsement deal with Nike worth $20 million per year, and when combined with his other endorsements, such as Gatorade, Hanes, and Rayovac, his non-salary earnings rose to $45 million per year in his last year of play (Spiegel, 1998).

Tiger Woods signed a contract with Nike immediately following his final amateur match. The five-year, $40 million Nike contract was one of the most lucrative in sport endorsement history. In addition, Titleist secured Woods as a spokesperson for five years at an estimated $20 million. His other early arrangements included $2 million from Rolex and $3 million per year from American Express. After winning the 1997 Master's, he also signed an agreement with Electronic Arts for a video game bearing his name that remains a top seller today. Tiger Woods renegotiated his contracts after the 2000 season (PGA Championship, US Open, British Open, Canadian Open) for a $100-million, five-year contract from Nike and one from Buick totaling $40 million [2004–2009] (Isidore, 2004a). Woods still ranked number one in 2008 with $128 million in total earnings ($22.9 million in winnings and $105 million in endorsements). His major sponsors included Gatorade, Buick, TAG Heuer, Gillette, EA Sports, and Accenture [global management and technology company] (Freedman, 2008).

Is he worth it? The financial data would seem to support the investment. 2004 Nike golf sales were estimated at $500 million, up 500% from 1997 (Isidore, 2004a). In the 2005 Master's, many remember Woods' chip shot that rolled ever-so-slowly to the lip of the cup to display the Nike logo on the ball for what seemed like an eternity. Within three weeks, Nike's total annual production of golf balls was sold out (Fullerton, 2007). Nike golf representative Dean Stoyer said, "Nobody can move product like Tiger can" (Isidore, 2004a, p. 5).

Woods is clearly the leader in athlete endorsements. 88% of Americans know of him, and 39% rank him as their favorite athlete (Isidore, 2004a). However, the influence of celebrity endorsers has been debatable. One survey showed only 4% of consumers said it was very important that a famous person endorsed a product (Schlossberg, 1990). Other data indicated that over 50% of the public thought athletes did it just for the money (Veltri, 1996). Furthermore, Veltri's research (1996) indicated that, with the exception of Michael Jordan (and assuredly now Woods), few people were able to match an athlete endorser and the products that he or she endorsed. In general, basketball players were more often accurately recognized than athletes in other sports, and male endorsers were more likely to be recognized than were female athletes (Veltri, 1996).

In the shadow of Jordan, rising star LeBron James signed agreements for over $100 million in endorsements during his 2004 rookie season, most notably from his seven-year, $90 million contract with Nike. James signed a variety of deals, including Coca-Cola for their Sprite and PowerAde brands (McCarthy, 2003). Bubblicious gum also signed James to a multiyear contract citing James' long-time loyalty and use of the chewing gum. James' 2008 earnings totaled $40.4 million (Freedman, 2008).

Endorsement earnings are not restricted to the U.S. market. International soccer superstar David Beckham lead the 2008 list with just over $48 million, followed by Formula 1 driver Kimi Räikkönen, who reportedly earned $46 million. It may be of interest to note that Formula 1 drivers own the sponsorship rights to their helmet, whereas the team owner has the rights to signage on the car and the driver's uniform. Unfortunately for the driver trying to leverage a substantial fee, research shows that only 6% of the exposure value comes from the driver's helmet. Thirty-three percent comes from the car, and 24% comes from the driver's suit. Others on the list included Brazilian soccer star Ronaldinho of FC Barcelona, who made $37.5 million and tennis star Roger Federer, who made $35.1 million. Unfortunately, few women made the list of top endorsers. Maria Sharapova was ranked 13th on the international list with earnings of $21.8 million (Freedman, 2008). Golfer Lorena Ochoa of Mexico was also a top endorsement leader with over $10 million in income, mostly from Mexican national corporations (Pitoniak, 2008).

Endorsement opportunities are not limited to traditional sports. Seven-time Tour De France champion Lance Armstrong's endorsement earnings total $16 million annually and ranges from Trek bicycles and Coke to Subaru motorcars. Extreme sports, like snowboarding and motor-cross, also present athletes with endorsements. Skateboarder Tony Hawk began the sport's revolution with reported earnings of more than $10 million in 2003 from his products, most significantly from his Pro Skater video game. At that time, it was the number one sports video game and number three seller of all video games. Shaun White, 2006 Olympic Gold medalist and multiple X-Games champion, signed a multimillion dollar deal with Burton snowboards in 2008 ("Shaun White and Burton sign," 2008).

In this age of technology, the opportunities for endorsements and licensing of players and players' names have evolved from traditional trading cards to video game licensing rights. Basic licensing agreements are typically managed by players associations. MLB and the NFL have separate programs run through their respective unions, the Major League Baseball Players Association (MLBPA) and the National

Football League Players Association (NFLPA). The National Basketball Association Players Association (NBAPA) granted all rights to the NBA for $25 million per year plus $8 million for use of the NBAPA logo. In 2006, the NFLPA earned $19.5 million just from trading cards to produce a total income of $109 million. In the NFL, each player received $48,000 a year in addition to a percentage based on the sale of player-identified items, such as jerseys, posters, and bobbleheads. NFL players receive 10% on player-identified items, but the MLBPA must also pay the league a 15% royalty for use of team names and logos on its deals, as is the case with trading cards, video games, and commercials etc., if team uniforms and logos are used (Kaplan, 2008).

In 2008, MLBPA brought in $16.8 million with another $6.2 million from the league for logo use. Each MLB player received $33, 675.03 in 2006 from licensing revenues. EA Sports paid the NFL Players Association $35.1 million in 2008 in licensing rights for games, such as Madden NFL 09, with $7,500 going to each player based on video game licensing (Kaplan, 2008).

Controversies

Controversies surfaced during the 1992 Olympic Games when the USA men's basketball team won the gold medal. Several members of the "Dream Team" had endorsement contracts with Nike, yet Reebok had supplied the US Olympic Committee with its presentation uniforms. Just prior to the medal ceremony, some team members refused to display the Reebok logo during the medal presentations. A compromise was reached wherein players who objected could open the collars of their uniform to cover the logo or drape a U.S. flag over the offending logo. For 1998, the USOC established new, more restrictive, guidelines for logos on team apparel and revised their athlete-participation agreement. The code of conduct introduced for the Athens 2004 Games prohibited athletes from "concealing or covering up a USOC sponsor, supplier, or licensee brand of other identification" (Lombardo, 2004, p. 5). Further complications arose at the 2008 Beijing Olympic Trials when multi-gold medalist U.S. swimmer Michael Phelps was barred from wearing a sponsor's logo on his swim cap. Previously in the 2004 Trials, Phelps and other swimmers had been allowed to have sponsor logos on their caps (Mickle, 2008).

The twist comes over the controlling body associated with the Olympic Trials. Although U.S. Swimming conducts the Trials, it does so under the auspices of the USOC. U.S. Swimming claimed that, although their rules had precluded cap logos other than the manufacturer, they had not previously enforced the rule. The USOC, in a position of control, demanded strict adherence to the USOC restrictions (Mickle, 2008).

At the international level, the IOC restrictions in place for Beijing 2008 indicate that "no identification other than the manufacturer's logo may appear on any clothing, equipment, or accessories. Pursuant to Rule 53 By-law 1.4 of the Olympic Charter, one identification of the manufacturer per clothing item will be permitted with a maximum size of 20 cm^2" (IOC, 2006).

Another Beijing-related issue arose when the coach of the US Olympic Swim team, Mark Schubert, commented that, if you weren't wearing the new Speedo LZR swimsuit, "you'd probably be at home watching the Olympics on NBC." This prompted a law suit from TYR, who manufactured a competing suit, citing undue pressure on athletes to wear only Speedo, the USA Swimming sponsor, suits. U.S. Swimming commented that, the last time they checked, the United States was a country with freedom of speech and Coach Schubert was free to express his opinion (Henderson, 2008, p. 16C).

There are issues regarding the potential endorsement of women as sex objects. It has been reported that "some elite beach female volleyballers have had their breasts enlarged, and others over-train their stomach muscles in an effort to obtain the hard, rippled abdomen now touted by the fitness industry as the sexy in-look for women. The intent for both of these body-sculpturing strategies is to use sex appeal to attract an audience to the contests and to attract commercial sponsorship and endorsement contracts" (Brooks, 2001, p. 1). In the early 2000s, tennis player Anna Kournikova was at the center of the controversy. While near the top of women's tennis, she was able to secure endorsements from a variety of companies, but in the process, she began focusing more on her modeling career than tennis and dropped out of the world rankings. Her endorsements, however, continued to rise and seemed to be based predominately on her attractiveness. Her reported earnings exceeded $15 million per year. One of her endorsements was for British company Berlei's Shock Absorber Multiway Sports Bra, a number one seller in Britain, and featured the ad line, "Only the ball should bounce" (McCarthy, 2003). This clearly crossed the line from athleticism to sexism. Fink, Kensicki, Fitzgerald, and Brett (2004) referred to this type of endorsement as "hyper-sexualized." In their research, they investigated whether a woman's attractiveness or expertise would more effectively influence consumers. Their findings showed that expertise was more effective in establishing a fit between the athlete and the product and, therefore, would better influence consumers. In related research, Brooks (2001) noted, "Marketers using a sexual appeal approach find it very difficult to determine how consumers will interpret this type of message"(p. 3). Brooks contends that "promoting sport by using the female players as a sexual impulse stimulus may not be a profitable, long-term course for either the sport or for the sponsors" (p. 8). As an aside, the use of athletes as sex objects has not been restricted to women. In 2008, soccer start David Beckham was signed by fashion designer Giorgio Armani to endorse its new line of underwear through quite provocative commercials.

Unfortunately, women make considerably less than their male counterparts in sport endorsements. The 2007 endorsement leader in women's sport was tennis' Maria Sharapova, who earned a reported $23 million per year (Jackson, 2007). This included a 10-year, $25 million deal with Prince racquets. The highest women's individual endorsement contract to-date was secured by tennis player Venus Williams, who signed a five-year, $40 million deal with Reebok in 2000. Her sister Serena signed an agreement with Nike in 2003 for a total of $60 million over eight years (Glase, 2003). Both sisters average about $15 million per year in off-court earnings with those earnings projected to increase after their 2008 Wimbledon finals match. Another leader in endorsement earnings was golf star Annika Sorenstam, who reportedly made over $8 million in 2007 endorsement earnings just prior to her 2008 retirement. Although not on the 2008 list, race driver Danica Patrick is sure to make the 2009 rankings. With her first Indycar victory and substantial press coverage, 2008 and 2009 should be banner years for her.

Almost all sports organizations have so-called "billboard" rules regulating the size of sponsor logos that appear on uniforms. The NCAA, NFL, NBA, MLB, and NHL all have such legislation. The IOC does as well, but a lesson was learned by the IOC at the 1988 Seoul Olympics: It limited the size of logos on swimming touch pads, starting blocks, and timing devices but not the number of logos. Consequently, timing sponsor Seiko literally covered its equipment with tiny little logos. There was also a dispute over tattoos as advertising. In 2001, boxer Bernard Hopkins entered the ring with a corporate logo for GoldenPalace.com tattooed on his back. Although it was not prohibited in the existing rules, the Nevada State Athletic Commission acted quickly to enact legislation to prohibit such actions in the future. In another incident, NBA player Rasheed Wallace entertained an offer from a candy company to place a temporary tattoo on his bicep. Wallace declined the offer, but NBA commissioner David Stern commented that, "although NBA rules did not specifically prohibit body billboards, . . . its rules and restrictions with respect to both player endorsements and commercial logos on uniforms would enable the league to prevent Wallace from wearing a temporary tattoo featuring a corporate logo" (McKelvey, 2003, p. 3). However, it seems that body logos are on everyone at beach volleyball matches.

In 2007, the NFL stepped up its enforcement of league logo policies: "The League has gone so far as to threaten NFL club equipment managers with fines if players on their teams wear equipment that does not comply with NFL rules. At each game, an NFL inspector will be present to make sure that policies are being followed" (Kaplan, 2007, p. 5).

Exceptions, however, have been made. MLB, as noted above, has a rule prohibiting commercial logos on uniforms but has suspended that rule when teams played in Japan. In 2004, the New York Yankees and the Tampa Bay Devil Rays wore "Ricoh" patches on their sleeves, and in 2008, the world champion Boston Red Sox sported "EMC," a data storage company, patches on their sleeves.

The dispute over logos has not been confined to team sports. During the 1998 US Open in tennis, Venus Williams was fined $100 by the Women's Tennis Association (WTA) for refusing to wear the Corel WTA Tour patch on her clothing. Williams cited her Reebok contract language which "prohibited any other logo" on her dress (Kaplan, 1998, p. 9). Interestingly, the WTA rules allowed an exemption for Nike. Williams threatened to sue but ultimately acquiesced. Reebok stayed above the fray, saying that Williams could do whatever she wanted to do (Kaplan, 1998). In 2003, the ATP relaxed its restrictions on logos. The previous rule was that a player could not wear a non-apparel logo on the front of a shirt, specifically in the case of VISA. If a player had a Nike logo on the front, the player had to put the ATP logo on the back. The modification to the rule allowed non-apparel logos and apparel logos and did not require the ATP logo. However, the four Grand Slam events to date still prohibit non-apparel logos on player shirts. McKelvey noted that these instances "illustrate a growing tension between the desire and the need of sport organizations to regulate and control their business and players, versus the individual freedoms of players, particularly with respect to their pursuit of commercial endorsements" (McKelvey, 2003, p. 3).

The issue of control is so contentious that officials initiated a lawsuit against the NCAA. In 1998, adidas filed suit against the NCAA because it restricted advertising logos by manufacturers, yet allowed its own logos and sport conferences and football bowl sponsors' logos to exceed the standards. In 2004, several jockeys went to court and won the right to sell advertising on their silks. "I know that there are people who fear that jockeys will now look like logo-covered NASCAR drivers, ruining the majesty and tradition of the Run for the Roses. But if tradition-rich events like the Masters can survive Tiger Woods and the Nike hype machine, the Sport of Kings can withstand a few dollars trickling down to the peasants" (Isidore, 2004b). Jockeys, unless they finish in the top three, can go home with as little $56 for a race.

Agents and Agencies	Marketing agents are typically the individuals responsible for assisting athletes in obtaining sponsorships and product endorsements. However, many athletes have other related business and marketing needs. These could include personal appearances and speaking engagements, appearances on screen and in television, print advertising, and investment management. Few individual agents could competently furnish all of the services cited above. Therefore, several companies have been established to offer athletes a package of services from experts in each area. These firms not only represent athletes but provide marketing and sponsorship services, as well as ownership of many major events. Globally, there are other firms engaged in the business as well. Overall, since 2005, there has been a merger of sport representation and celebrity representation in agencies like the Creative Artists Agency (CAA). Since 2007, the CAA has been hiring some of the top athletes' agents and is aggressively pursuing more sport clients. And by 2008, they were the top ranked agency in terms of players' salaries. For example, they not only represent Tom Cruise, Brad Pitt, and Cameron Diaz but also Peyton Manning, Derek Jeter, and the ultimate duo, David and Victoria Beckham. The industry is not, however, free from problems. Another entertainment giant, Wasserman Media Groups, is also moving rapidly into athlete representation. IMG has its root in tennis and golf, since Arnold Palmer in the 1960s, and represents players such as Tiger Woods and Natalie Gulbis in golf, as well as Maria Sharipova and Roger Federer in tennis. Octagon scored big in 2008, representing Olympic swimmer Michael Phelps and his eight gold medal performances. To enable the reader to get a more thorough understanding of agent representation, a sample agent-athlete contract for management has been included at the end of this chapter.

Agent fees can run as high as 5–15% on marketing and endorsement projects. However, U.S. professional leagues' players associations generally restrict agent fees on playing contracts to 3%. The key questions to be asked are: what monies are the percentage of fees calculated from and is the money paid on salary actually paid to the player or to the total value of the negotiated contract?

In fairness to sports agents, most of them do safeguard the best interests of their players. In fact, they often are more knowledgeable about the player's worth than the player, and they have a working knowledge of the types of performance provisions that can go into a player's contract. In the final analysis, agents will be better at negotiating the contract than the athlete.

Trends

Although there is some sentiment regarding famous players, both team and individual, as effective product endorsers and corporate spokespersons, there are some indicators that the times may be changing. Many of the leading sport shoe manufacturers downsized their endorsement contracts in the late 1990s. For example, in 1995, Reebok had 130 NBA players under endorsement contracts but reduced the number to 10 by 1998 (Lombardo, 1998). Although reports suggest the reduction was based on changes in company revenues, some suggested that "brat-like" attitudes and consumer indifference were more likely the cause. Similarly, Nike cut endorsement spending considerably due to a downturn in market conditions and sales (Mullen, 1998), yet terms and payments rebounded in the mid 2000s. The trend also reached into other sport industries: "Following the trend that saw sneaker companies slash endorsement contracts, major US golf club manufacturers suffering from sagging sales were cutting back on the number of golfers they pay to carry their clubs" (Mullen, 1998, p. 3).

Companies began to question the credibility and integrity of athlete endorsers in the 1990s. This questioning was accentuated by indiscretions and criminal acts by such personalities as boxing champion Mike Tyson and NBA player Latrell Sprewell. Tyson was imprisoned for assault, and Sprewell attempted to strangle his coach at a team practice. A few years later Sprewell was said to have told his team owners, "Just tell me how much you are going to fine me for not showing up at your required personal appearances and I'll write you a check." Under the NBA collective bargaining agreement and standard player contract, NBA players must make six personal appearances as requested by the team—similar situations still arise today.

Although not criminal in nature, other athletes' actions also embarrass event organizers and sponsors. 2008 FIS World Cup Alpine Ski champion Bode Miller has presented a variety of challenges for his sponsors. After Miller failed to medal in the 2006 Olympics, several sponsors dropped him as a spokesperson. This was not necessarily based on his performance but on comments made to the media about skiing drunk. For the 2007 to 2008 Season Miller formed his own support group independent from the US Ski Team, known as "Team Bode." However, FIS rules required him to wear the official uniform of the US Ski Team in competitions. Some sponsors were excited to be associated with Miller without having to pay the fee, while others were frightened that they would be caught in difficult situations even though they were not officially affiliated with Miller.

In response to these situations, many endorsement contracts now include special clauses to cover instances where a player or coach is involved in some scandal that reflects negatively on the sponsor. Some contracts reserve the right to terminate an agreement at any time if the commercial value of the endorsee is substantially impaired by the commission of any act that tends to denigrate, insult, or offend the community standards of public morale and decency (Hein, 2003).

In reaction to this scenario, some corporations are turning increasingly to outstanding women athletes for their endorsement options. "Today's crop of women's sports standouts is, for the most part, more accessible than their male counterparts. They will autograph posters and spend time to motivate young fans" (Rodin, 1998, p. 34). They are also less likely to behave in immoral and unethical ways that might embarrass the company. Stone et al. (2003) noted, "Our study suggests that endorsement opportunities for female athletes are growing and that elite female athletes may now be able to effectively compete with male athletes for some of the lucrative endorsement deals that have traditionally gone to men" (p. 101). The trend is reasonably clear: companies are looking for "squeaky clean" images, and today's women athletes seem to fit the ticket (Gatlin, 2003).

Another reaction to what one author (Cordiner, 2002) dubbed as the "Tyson Factor" has been to seek team and event sponsorships rather than individual athletes, signaling a future trend. Teams and events were determined by sponsors to have more longevity than players and, thus, are more able to provide extended market influence. Volvo's Smart Sponsoring checklist also produces additional support by suggesting that companies should "put money into the sport itself and events linked with it. Not in individual athletes" ("Volvo and Sport Sponsorship," 1990, p. 5).

However, just to prove that events are not completely risk free, the 2002 Olympic Games came under U.S. Justice Department investigation for offering bribes to IOC members and their families in an effort obtain the rights to host the Games. Several sponsors, including Qwest Communications, commented that they were "disappointed in the recent events, the negative press in general surrounding the Olympic movement, and the 'lessening of value' of our substantial commitment" (Finley, 1998, p. 15A).

Irrespective of the problems associated with athlete endorsements, these individual sponsorship arrangements can be effective in marketing products and services in the sport industry. A worksheet for marketing an individual athlete has been included at the end of the chapter. Brooks and Harris (1998) suggested that the most effective endorsements are those that contain a high level of consistency between the image of the endorser and the product or service image. In fact, Boyd and Shank's research (2004) on the effectiveness of endorsements indicated that athletes were most effective when specifically endorsing sports products. This concept supports the contention of McDonald (1998) presented in Chapter 3 and research on the effectiveness of endorsements (Boyd & Shank, 2004) that carefully match sponsorship and corporate personality as a critical relationship.

SAMPLE
Personal Financial Management Contract

This agreement is made this _____ day of _____ , 20___ , by and between
_____ , hereinafter "Player," and _____ , hereinafter "Manager."
In consideration of the promises made by each to the other, Player and Manager
agree as follows:

1. FINANCIAL MANAGEMENT SERVICES—Manager hereby warrants and
   represents to Player that he holds college degrees in Business Administration
   and Law from accredited universities, with sufficient hours of study in Ac-
   counting and Marketing to qualify as majors in both fields, and that he has
   limited experience and training in investments. Player hereby retains Manager
   to advise, counsel, and assist Player in the management of income generated
   through Player's occupation as a professional athlete. Manager, serving in a fi-
   duciary capacity, shall act in such manner as to protect the best interest of
   Player and assure effective representation of Player in matters directly and in-
   directly related to Player's financial situation. Manager shall not have authority to bind or commit Player to enter into any contract or agreement without
   actual execution thereof by the Player.

   Manager shall provide financial management services to the Player as follows: (i) tax planning and preparation of federal and state income tax returns;
   (ii) assisting Player in determining a satisfactory budget of Player's income on
   a monthly and yearly basis; (iii) assisting Player in establishing investment
   goals; (iv) assisting Player in evaluating investment opportunities proposed to
   Player; (v) assisting Player in securing duly qualified professionals for legal, ac-
   counting, estate planning, investment, and insurance services as Player may
   desire or need.

   In the event Manager shall be able to provide professional services set out in
   (v) above, he must provide said services at the normal rate charged to his
   clients in said area of professional expertise.

2. FINANCIAL MANAGER'S COMPENSATION—For services provided to
   the Player pursuant to the terms of Paragraph 1 of this Agreement, above,
   Player shall pay to Manager an amount that, when added to fees paid to Manager pursuant to the Agreement to represent Player in contract negotiations
   that was executed on _____ , 20___ , shall equal three per cent
   (3%) of Player's gross income from base salary, signing bonus, reporting
   bonus, and squad bonus as set forth in his Player's contract for the year in
   which services are performed, payable as received by the Player from his club.

3. INVESTMENT SERVICES—Manager agrees to keep Player informed of
   any investment opportunities which the Manager feels may be beneficial to
   the Player. In the event that the Manager shall secure an investment opportu-

nity for the Player that the Player desires to acquire, he shall keep accurate statements as to the condition of said investment and shall report said conditions to the Player no less frequently than every three months, or, if information is not available at such intervals, immediately upon receipt of a status report from the record-keeping source of said investment.

Player may, at his discretion, empower Manager to exercise all rights of ownership with regards to the investments made by Manager on behalf of Player by executing written documents that specifically set out the powers given to Manager by Player for such matters as collection of income, purchase of additional interests in each said investment, or sale or transfer of said investment.

4. COMPENSATION—Player shall pay to Manager a sum equal to five percent (5%) of the appreciation in value, income received, whether ordinary or capital gain, for each investment made by Manager on behalf of Player.

   For purposes of this Paragraph, investments made for Player by a qualified and licensed investment broker secured by Manager for Player shall not be considered to be made by the Manager, and Player shall not be liable for compensation to Manager for income or appreciation in value of said investments.

5. PERSONAL APPEARANCE SERVICES—Manager shall use his best efforts to assist Player in enhancing Player's public image and in assisting Player in securing personal appearances, such as, but not limited to, speaking engagements, commercial endorsements, autograph sessions, promotions, licensing arrangements, and appearances in any mass media outlet. Player shall use such efforts as are reasonably necessary to appear at said opportunities and to improve speaking and related talents so as to provide a good public image for himself and the organization for which he is appearing.

6. COMPENSATION—For all types of public appearance opportunities secured for Player by the Manager, the Player shall pay to the Manager a sum equal to fifteen percent (15%) of the gross income received by Player for each said appearance. For purposes of public appearance opportunities only, Manager shall be responsible for expenses incurred by him in attempting to secure said opportunities for Player, unless Player agrees in writing to reimburse Manager for expenses incurred on Player's behalf in these matters.

7. EXPENSES—Except as provided in Paragraph 6 above, Player shall reimburse Manager for all expenses that are reasonable and necessary in providing the services on Player's behalf as set out in this Agreement upon receipt of an itemized statement of said expenses from Manager to the Player.

8. ENTIRE AGREEMENT—This Agreement sets forth the entire agreement between the parties hereto and replaces or supersedes all prior agreements between the parties related to the same subject matter. This Agreement cannot be changed orally.

9. TERM—This agreement shall remain in full force and effect for a period of one year from the date above or until the final contract negotiated by Manager for Player with a professional athletic team has expired, whichever shall last occur. However, Player and Manager shall have the right to terminate this

Agreement with written notice delivered personally, or by regular United States mail, to the party at his last-known address and upon the payment of all fees and expenses due hereunder by the terminating party to the other party.

10. GOVERNING LAW—This Agreement shall be construed, interpreted, and enforced according to the laws of the State of _____ .

EXAMINE THIS CONTRACT CAREFULLY

BEFORE SIGNING IT

IN WITNESS WHEREOF, the parties hereto have hereunto signed their names as hereinafter set forth.

_____   _____

AGENT   PLAYER

The worksheets provide a guide for you in developing various sections of a sponsorship plan. The following sheets cover areas that must be addressed when attempting to secure endorsements for individual athletes. Complete this worksheet as you would prepare a sponsorship plan.

Individual Athlete Sponsorship Worksheets

Specify the image, personal likes and dislikes, and speaking abilities of your athlete.

_____
_____
_____
_____
_____
_____
_____
_____
_____
_____
_____

Prepare a list of the products currently used by your athlete.

_____
_____
_____
_____
_____

Identify possible value-in-kind (VIK) opportunities.

_____
_____

_____

Report the specific sport-imposed time constraints that would affect endorsement appearances.

_____

Calculate the relative value of your athlete compared to other athletes.

_____

Brainstorm tentative corporations that could be targeted for consideration.

_____

Research the most likely corporations for approach.

_____

Assemble an "Athlete Package," including a cover letter, athlete biography, photographs, previous endorsements, and family background.

_____

Establish a calendar for presenting or mailing packages to potential corporations and set your allowable response timeline.

_____

_____

_____

_____

_____

Create a checklist to track the results of your efforts.

_____

_____

_____

_____

_____

Chapter Six

FINANCIAL IMPLICATIONS

Introduction

The finances involved in sports sponsorships are staggering. As mentioned in the first chapter of this workbook, worldwide spending on sponsorship was estimated to be $43 billion in 2008. It's also important to remember that not all sponsorship arrangements involve the exchange of cash. Successful sponsorships often involve trading goods and services that a corporation controls and the sport organization may need. This has generally been termed "value-in-kind" (VIK), and on average, 40% of all sponsorship agreements encompass at least some provision involving the supply of products and services. Several examples have been presented throughout this workbook. Colleges and universities trade sponsorship and signage for uniforms and shoes; the Olympics accepts computers and data processing in return for sponsorship; and many road races accept energy drinks in return for on-course signage. It is important, however, to heed the words of Mike Mushett, an executive with the 1996 Paralympic Games: "You can't meet payroll with M&M's and Coke" (Mushett, 1995).

What sponsors are looking for is a positive return on their investments. Dannon calculated a positive return on their sponsorship of the Dannon Duathlon Championship Series. Partnering with local grocery stores in each of the eight yearly events, Dannon was able to generate $750,000 from their $250,000 investment ("Dannon sponsorship," 2003). Ukman (2004) also provided a breakout of calculating ROI for a boat show that is included at the end of this chapter as a Best Practice.

While many sponsors are demanding a clearer ROI, many experts in the industry are more focused on ROO (return-on-objective). At a 2008 summit on Sponsorship Measurement, Elizabeth Lindsey, senior VP at the Wasserman Media Group, said that sport sponsorship will never have one standard measure for ROI/ROO but that shouldn't stop disciplined evaluation (Lindsay, 2008). Skildum-Reid (2008a) suggests that "there are some things that can be measured in dollars but most can't. The newest thinking on sponsorship measurement is to shift to the ROO model" (p. 5). This model suggests that corporations establish a budget for the accomplishment involved in specified sponsorship objectives. This would fit nicely with hospitality objectives that are difficult to measure on a dollar-to-dollar basis.

Details of the sponsorship agreement between adidas and the Tampa Bay Buccaneers may provide insight to the seldom-seen financial side of sponsorships (Friedman, 1999, p. 36.) The Tampa Bay Buccaneers put together sponsorship packages for their new adidas-sponsored stadium. Through a five-year, $1.7 million agreement, adidas agreed to provide $4.4 million in products and $675,000 for community outreach programs. The package included, among other items:

1) two 22-by-28-foot trivision panels on each scoreboard,

2) one corporate identification (five feet high) above the lower suite level,

3) inclusion of the corporate logo in one 16-by-40-foot themed mural in the main stadium concourse,

4) signs at six novelty stands,

5) one sponsor identification on the score board per quarter of play,

6) two full-page advertisements in *NFL Insider Magazine*,

7) periodic mentions in the Buccaneers' newsletter,

8) ability to place promotional flyers in stadium cup holders for each game,

9) presence on team's Internet homepage,

10) one 16-person luxury suite,

11) 70 season tickets for all home games (i.e., 10 in club section and 60 in preferred general admission seating sections),

12) 16 tickets for the Super Bowl,

13) four parking passes,

14) one catered tailgate party for 100 guests,

15) VIP day for 20 guests at one practice session during the season, and

16) one away-game trip per season for four guests (Freidman, 1999).

In this package, no elements were priced individually but rather bundled together with a total price for all components.

Pricing Sponsorships

The first thing the sport marketer needs to know about pricing a sponsorship is that nobody cares how much money your sport organization needs. Sponsorship consultant Kim Skildum-Reid (2008b, p. 9) said, "The money you need to run an event has nothing to do with its commercial value. Got it? Nothing." Sponsors only care about the value they can get from the partnership. Several different approaches to sponsorship pricing have been utilized extensively in the industry. The following sections address the three most commonly used methods for sponsorship pricing as outlined by Brooks (1994).

COST-PLUS METHOD

In this technique, you calculate the actual expenses incurred in providing the sponsorship package plus a desired profit for the organization. Costs include all items, such as tickets, parking, dinners, souvenirs, and signage. This method has been used effectively by the USOC to price their sponsorship packages. In using this method, be sure to include the labor costs associated with the production of the above elements. In this manner, you will be able to demonstrate to senior management the true profits of the organization.

COMPETITIVE MARKET STRATEGY

As with any product pricing strategy, you must be competitive with alternative sponsorship options; the problem is trying to discover their price. In the sponsorship business, it is difficult to know the pricing structure of competitors' packages. One of the best ways is to read prominent trade publications. The leading publication on sport sponsorship is the *IEG Sponsorship Report*. This biweekly newsletter covers all of the major activity in the sponsorship industry and includes interviews with industry leaders. For example, the newsletter tracks worldwide spending and reports trends in North America, as well as around the globe. Another noteworthy publication is *SportsBusiness Journal*. Although this weekly publication does not focus solely on sport sponsorship, it does present a variety of articles on the topic. The *IEG Sponsorship Report* systematically lists the prices of all major sponsorship signing on a quarterly basis.

RELATIVE VALUE METHOD

This approach to pricing is based on the market value of each sponsorship component. For example, if you are including souvenir program ads in your sponsorship package, you could compare this component to the price and effectiveness of ads in the newspaper. Scoreboard signage could be valued against the cost of billboards, and PA announcements could be equated with radio advertising. You will need to ascertain if the comparison is legitimate and if the same impact can be achieved. This can be accomplished through a review of the cost per thousand (CPM; "M" representing the Roman numeral for 1,000). Even if your CPM turns out to be higher, you might argue that your audience has a better demographic match to a particular group than it would match the mass media. It has been reported that event-based media elements are somewhat less effective than a direct advertising message. Their suggested value is about 20% of the media cost; however, if the events are provided actual advertising spots during event television broadcasts and legitimate advertising space from a media sponsor, the value would be equal to the full rate offered to other advertisers (Stotlar, 2001; Ukman, 2004).

Grey and Skildum-Reid (2007) suggested that the ratio of media sponsorship should range from 3:1 to 8:1, with more value placed on the media partner than on the cost. Another suggestion indicates that the sponsorship should provide a point of differentiation for the media outlet from their competitors. You should also work within the negotiation process to retain control of the advertising schedule.

In an effort to help event owners justify return on investment to sponsors, one company, Joyce Julius & Associates, has been providing support data for more than 20 years. Their concept was to tabulate the total time that a sponsor's logo appeared on television coverage of major events and then to provide an exposure value based on the cost of airing a 30-second commercial during the same period. For example, data from the 2008 Daytona 500 indicated that ALLTEL was the sponsor receiving the largest exposure value. As the sponsor of Ryan Newman's winning car, ALLTEL logos were seen on screen for a total of 17 minutes, which valued at more than $18 million. Placement of the logos is also critical. Many sponsors agree that the best way to advertise in NASCAR is to put their logo on the hood or rear quarter panels of a winning driver's car. However, even companies like 3M generated $8 million in exposure value from a fender decal. Data from the 2008 bowl games showed logo placement on the 20-yard line outperformed midfield logos 4-to-1. Allstate Insurance, who sponsored both the Sugar Bowl and the BCS Title Championship game, received more than $230 million in value from almost two hours of on-screen exposure (Joyce Julius, 2008). The 2008 NBA Champion Boston Celtics petitioned the NBA to change restrictions on court-side signage such that the 30-foot center court signage could be broken into two 10-foot signs at each end of the floor, and on the 25-foot center scores table sign. Their research indicated that, because most of the play occurs at the end of the courts, television exposure would increase by 250% (Lombaro, 2008).

In 2008, Nielsen Sports launched a service called "Nielsen Sponsorship Scorecard" to compete with Joyce Julius. They followed the same process but extended the concept to cover on screen logos and signage that appeared in sports news broadcasts like ESPN's SportCenter. Some have argued that the same advertising message can not be delivered in on-screen logo presence as it can be presented in a 30-second ad. However, that rationale fails if "channel surfers" and TiVo users are accounted for because they don't watch the commercials but are exposed to in-event messages. Perhaps a smart strategy is to use a ratio to assess the value of such exposure. IEG suggests that sponsors apply a 1-to-5 ratio in decreasing the value for on-screen logo appearance versus the actual cost of the commercial (Ukman, 2004).

Sponsors have also been known to use all of these price valuation methods for analyzing proposed sponsorship packages. NationsBank's sport and event marketing vice president said, "When I receive a proposal, I do a payout analysis, putting dollars against each benefit the property is offering" (Goldberg, 1998, p. 29).

COLLATERAL SUPPORT

To sufficiently support a sport sponsorship, corporations must be willing to spend additional dollars promoting their involvement. Estimates vary among corporations on the amount of additional spending that will be required to increase visibility of the sponsorship and will be needed to activate consumers. The general rule is that a sponsor must be willing to spend at least an amount equal to the rights fee of their sponsorship to leverage the effect (Grey & Skildum-Reid, 2007). Nextel's $45 million-per-year title sponsorship of NASCAR included a sponsor commitment to spend a like amount on marketing their relationship (Rovell, 2004). Coca-Cola estimates its ratio as 5-to-1 spending $5.00 on promotions and advertising for every $1.00 it spends on sponsorship fees. AT&T spent six times the cost of their sponsorship to make their sponsorships "known to employees and felt by customers" (Ukman, 1998, p. 2). Other authorities recommend that, at a minimum, sponsors spend an amount at least equal to the sponsorship fee for promotion and leveraging (Bernstein, 1998; Stotlar, 2001). A sponsorship alone, which is without collateral support, will rarely produce the desired results. The partnership must be leveraged through all of the sponsor's and the organization's assets.

Small Budget Sponsorships

In most small companies or divisions, the budget doesn't include a spare $700,000 to get involved in high-priced sport sponsorships. However, several companies have been successful in low budget sponsorships that have produced good results. Even at the Olympic level, sponsors can get in for a modest amount of money. By sponsoring US Speedskating for the 2002 Winter Olympic Games, uniform sponsors were able to have their logo appear on the cover of *Sports Illustrated* when Casey Fitzrandolf won a gold medal in the 500m. A full-page color ad in *Sports Illustrated* costs over $200,000, but there is no price for the cover. In another example, Bavarian Coachworks, a company specializing in customized Porsches, spent only $40,000 to get prime ad placement on a racecar entering into 17 events. The shop owner credited the ad with increasing his business 60 to 70%, many times above the cost of the sponsorship. Local auto racing can be even cheaper, as some drivers will almost give ad space away just so they can look like "real" sponsored racers.

At some point, the sport marketer has to ask for money from the sponsor (more detail on specific strategies will be presented in Chapter 8). It's much easier if the marketer has presented the financial benefits in a clear and precise manner. The sport marketer provides a service, a true benefit that can be measured in dollars, and is not asking for a charity handout. One major problem occurs when the money is hypothetically put on the table. If a sponsor offers $3,000 for a $10,000 package, the sport marketer has to walk away. A good package will stand on its own merit. With this business approach and attitude, a positive response is likely. An effective sport marketer has the data to show that sport sponsorship doesn't cost—it pays.

BEST PRACTICE

The following example was constructed by IEG (Ukman, 2004, p. 4) as a best practice in calculating return on sponsorship. The scenario details the results for an automotive manufacturer's $50,000 sponsorship of a boat show in which the primary objective was to increase Sport Utility Vehicle (SUV) sales.

Boat show attendance . . . . = 40,000
Attendees who visited booth and picked-up test drive offer . . . . . . = 14,000
Booth visitors who visited dealer for a test drive (7%) . . . . = 980
Test drivers who purchased within a 12 month period (12%) . . . . = 118
Average profit per vehicle . . . . = $2,000
Gross profit from sponsorship . . . . = $236,000
Rights fees . . . . = $50,000
Production and promotion costs . . . . = $50,000
Net profit . . . . = $136,000
Return on investment . . . . = 136%

The worksheets provide a guide for you in developing various sections of a sponsorship plan. The following sheets cover the financial aspects of pricing a sponsorship. Complete this worksheet as you would prepare a sponsorship plan.

Calculate a price for your sponsorship using the cost-plus method.

_____
_____
_____
_____
_____
_____
_____
_____
_____
_____

Compare the market value of similar sponsorships with your cost-plus calculations above, and evaluate the need for any adjustments in pricing your sponsorship.

_____
_____
_____
_____
_____
_____
_____
_____
_____
_____

Complete a relative value calculation by examining the media and retail tie-in portions of your sponsorship (if applicable), and evaluate the need for any adjustments in pricing your sponsorship.

_____
_____
_____
_____
_____
_____
_____
_____
_____

Examine the needs that your organization may have for sponsor products or services, and prepare a list of possible value-in-kind (VIK) contributions and their appropriate value.

_____
_____
_____
_____
_____
_____
_____
_____
_____
_____

Chapter Seven

DEVELOPING SUCCESSFUL SPORT SPONSORSHIP PROPOSALS

Introduction

This chapter will present an overview and a conceptual model for development of sport sponsorship proposals derived from field-based applications. Specific examples and procedures will be examined and presented to you for use as models in building sponsorships for your sport organization.

Sport has proven its revenue potential as a marketing vehicle, and the sponsorship proposal is the essential element for this process. The task of the sport manager lies in presenting a proposal that specifically identifies sponsors' benefits and needs (discussed in Chapter 3); however, it cannot be stressed enough that corporations are looking for flexibility in proposals, not set bundles of components. One corporate executive commented, "Most properties package what they need to sell without thinking what has value for their partners" (Goldberg, 1998, p. 29). The preferable strategy carefully examines each sponsor and uncovers the requisite needs for each potential sponsor.

IEG Sponsorship Report is one of the best sources for accessing information on the inside operations of companies sponsoring sport events (referenced earlier in the workbook). This Chicago-based, biweekly publication from the International Events Group (IEG) provides detailed analyses of sponsorship packages and the attendant framework. They also frequently list requests for sponsorship proposals from a variety of corporations.

Getting information about potential sponsors is essential. If the company is a publicly traded company, it is required to file an annual report with the Securities and Exchange Commission (SEC). Annual reports filed with the SEC can be accessed through their website (www.sec.gov) and through the Public Register's Annual Report Service (www.prars.com). Each of these sources can provide valuable data for use in structuring a sponsorship proposal.

In an effort to deal with an increasing number of proposals, many corporations prefer the online submission of sponsorship proposals, and some corporations have developed specific criteria for proposals. A sample online proposal format has been modified from several online sites and provided in Figure 7.1. Other corporations will consider any reasonable format devised by the event or property owner. In addi-

Name of the Event

Event Management Contact

Name _____

Title _____

Address _____

Phone _____

FAX _____

Email _____

Event Management Experience

Event Location(s)

Venue

Descript of the Event

Image Match and Integration

Number of Events

One-time only _____

Series of events _____

Duration of the Event

Proposed date(s) _____

Audience Size

Audience Demographics

Gender profile _____

Percentage in Age Groups

Percentage in income _____
brackets

Ethnicity profile _____

Lifestyle characteristics _____
(AOI)

Media Profile (specify coverage under
contract, historical data, or projected
coverage)

TV _____

Newspaper _____

Radio _____

Promotional Plan (specify coverage type,
length, units, frequency, production
details, and sponsor's access)

TV _____

Newspaper _____

Radio _____

Website _____

Direct mail _____

Database _____

PR events _____

Live marketing _____
event(s)

Level of Sponsorship (title, presenting,
supplier, etc.)

Sponsorship Category, Parameters,
and Exclusivity

Former Sponsors (list company, category, level, and year)

Existing and Proposed Sponsors (list
company(s), category, and level; indicate if under contract or proposed)

Sponsorable Components and Benefits

Signage _____

Venue messaging _____

Tag to media advertising _____

Hospitality (suites, _____
tickets, passes, parking,
food and beverages)

Pre-event activities _____

In-event activities _____

On-site product trial _____

On-site display _____

On-site product sales _____

Ceremonies _____

Celebrity/athlete/VIP _____
access or appearance

Value-in-kind (VIK) _____
opportunities

Cross-promotion _____
opportunities

Licensing _____

Post-event activities _____

Other _____

Identified Measures for Evaluation
Report

Rationale (why and how each benefit is
appropriate fit to the sponsor)

Proposed Budget and Value of Benefits

Figure 7.1. Sponsorship Submission Format Model

tion, excerpts and sample wording from an authentic sponsorship proposal have been included at the end of the chapter in Best Practice.

The level of sophistication has increased as the industry has matured throughout the last 10 years. Accordingly, few "boilerplate" sponsorship proposals have been effective. In other words, in an effort to save time, some sport properties have attempted to create a boilerplate proposal to distribute to multiple sponsors. These boilerplates usually contain the entire inventory that the organization has collected from their sponsorship; however, little attention is given to molding this package into the right framework for the targeted corporation. A simple "cut and paste" approach is taken in order to generate as many proposals as possible. As Lauletta, director of sports and event marketing for Miller Brewing Company, said, "I still receive proposals with Coors and Heineken's names in place of Miller and it always amazes me how lazy someone can be" (Lauletta, 2003, p. 8). Recipients easily expose this generic approach, and the proposal is most likely discarded.

In putting together a sponsorship proposal, Ukman (1995) suggested several attributes that should be addressed in a quality sponsorship proposal. She emphasized that the proposal should promote benefits, not package features. Company executives are looking for promotional platforms that can effectively produce quantifiable advantages for the company. Therefore, the focus of the proposal should be on the sponsor's, not the property's, needs. Ukman indicated that too often the proposal spends an inordinate amount of space detailing why the organization needs the money or how important it is to stage the event.

"The successful proposal is tailored to the sponsor's business category. Boilerplate proposals do not work" (Ukman, 1995, p. 2). As discussed in Chapter 3, specific attributes of a proposal may meet the image needs of one company, but another company may need product sampling. The sport marketer should work hard to establish a pre-proposal meeting in an effort to determine the specific needs of their prospects. They must do their homework and have a high level of understanding about the potential sponsor in order to actively participate in a discussion of their needs. Only then can an effective sponsorship proposal be developed. The proposal should also explain how benefits can be leveraged through the sponsor's existing marketing programs to achieve extended impact. Finally, the best proposals communicate the advantages of alliances and strategic partnerships that will ultimately provide greater utility than either party could accomplish separately (Ukman, 1995).

Sponsorship Description

The first step in developing an outstanding sponsorship proposal is the description of the event or property offered by the organization. This includes the history, years of organizational operation, and structure of the sport enterprise. Major corporations want to know the kind of organization with which they are getting involved. As pointed out at the New York-based Sports Summit, "If we are going to sponsor an event, I want to see the financial history of the people putting things together. How much can they cover? Is this event really going to come off? I know this sounds stupid but too many people never ask that question. Those are the ones that get burned" (Macnow, 1989, p. 39).

As previously mentioned in Chapter 3, a match must be made between corporate objectives and the opportunities available through the sponsorship arrangement. Therefore, the objectives of the proposal must be clearly presented in relation to how the sponsorship will benefit the sponsor. Specific objectives must be delineated regarding target market demographics, psychographics, image opportunities, awareness strategies, market share increases, and business-to-business relationships.

Proposal Objectives and Match to Sponsor Needs

Just as marketing practices have changed from a product orientation to a market orientation, sponsorships have changed, as well. In the early days of sponsorship, properties would put together "Gold, Silver and Bronze" style packages and offer them to potential sponsors. Those days have long ago passed and the need for flexibility and customization is essential. All too often, properties are intent on selling their inventory of sponsorable components, rather than presenting options to a potential sponsor that the property needs. Respondents in Seaver's 2004 corporate survey advised marketers to align sponsorship proposals to meet the business objectives of prospective sponsors. Attention to these factors can result in a longstanding sponsorship association.

The available components of sponsorship should be presented to the sponsor in detail. Every available activity or planned event should be described, including the corporate opportunities available within each activity or event. These should be linked to standard business practices that have been proven to produce results. In addition, these results should be clearly tied to actionable components of the sponsorship. For example, most corporations have a positioning strategy in place. A proposal should describe how the features of the sponsorship could solidify the organization's corporate position in the mind of the consumer.

Sponsorable Components

A good place to start is to reexamine the needs for sponsors, presented in Chapter 3. When examing what sponsors want, the sport marketer will need to conduct an audit of the benefits that the organization has to offer. There are, of course, the natural elements surrounding the sport organization, such as stadium signage, the title of an event or activity, and the advertising linked the organization's communication outlets (e.g., game/event program ads, television, newspapers, and websites). However, with a little creativity, features like a newsletter and access to a customer database can really pull the sponsor into a sport organization and create a true partnership. It is recommended that if the organization doesn't already have a newsletter or customer database, the sport marketer should help to create one for them. Sport properties also have a great opportunity to assist with product displays and product sampling. As noted with the USA Swimming sponsorship by a sunscreen product, the manufacturer wanted to get its product into the hands of its target market. In another case, auto dealers were able to capitalize on grassy areas of the football stadium for vehicle display during their prime new model introduction period with no added costs for the organization. Other assets, like hospitality, inclusion in PR events, and permission to co-promote with your logo, are great additions to a sport marketer's inventory.

Sample Inventory

(adapted from Grey, A.M., & Skildum-Reid, K. (2007). *Sponsorship seekers toolkit* [2nd Ed.]. Sydney: McGraw Hill.)

Sponsorship Types

Title sponsor
Presenting sponsor
Naming rights (for awards, facility sections, subordinated event, or an entire day)
Official product or supplier

Exclusivity

At given levels
Within certain categories (define them clearly)

License and Endorsement

Use of event or team logo in their advertising
Official product status

On-site

Sampling opportunities
Product demonstrations and displays
On-site sales or merchandising

Signage

Venue locations (size and location specific)
Vehicles
Participant and/or staff uniforms or number tags
Flags or banners

Hospitality

Tickets to the event
VIP parking or shuttle service
Access to specified VIP areas
Access to specified VIP activities ("money cannot buy" experiences)
Customized VIP experiences and events

Technology

Banners and content on your website with links to their sites
Web-based promotional events

Loyalty Marketing

Special parking or access to their customers (e.g., several stadiums have Lexus parking zones)
Early access to tickets (e.g., American Express arranged this with tennis' US Open)
Access to special blocks of seating

Database Marketing

Access to event or organization database
Promotional flyers in event or organization mailings

One of the best features about sport is an inventory that cannot be duplicated by many other industries. Of course, sponsors can buy television exposure and ads in newspapers and magazines, but they can't buy access to players and coaches or behind the scenes tours in sport venues. Cannon, who has been a long-standing NFL sponsor, has found a high level of success with its "Shoot Like a Pro" program. Amateur photographers enter the contest on Cannon's (or the NFL team's) website for a chance to win game tickets and sideline passes for a selected game. Photos are taken with the latest Cannon camera, and the amateur gets tips from a professional photographer. It provides a great experience for the contestants and truly enhances the Cannon brand. In 2004, one of the sponsors of the Denver Grand Prix, an auto dealership, was able to offer a lap around the racecourse for any customer who bought a new vehicle during the promotional period. These are benefits that were created especially for specific sponsors. It was creative and effective and had no added sponsorship costs.

Sports teams also have the benefit of providing access to "game used" items, like game-worn jerseys and game balls for sponsors. Although there is a cost related to providing these items, it can easily be offset through the price of the sponsorship. These special benefits are an important part of a sport marketer's inventory. They create meaning for the fans and help transfer the emotion from the sport to the sponsor. Also, when a sport marketer combines sponsorable components, they must truly differentiate those components that fall under higher levels of sponsorship from those in lower categories. Multiple factors and components differentiating a $100,000 from a $50,000 sponsorship should be considered; for example, the $100,000 sponsorship should produce more than just twice as many stadium signs.

It is also essential that the responsibility for developing each aspect should be clarified. If corporate hospitality is a primary feature of the proposal, who will provide the catering must be verified. Typically, the event or property provides the facility and arranges the dialog with approved caterers. Ultimately, it is the sponsor who selects the menu and finalizes the service protocol and details.

Pricing

The presentation of cost estimates has been an area where many sports organizations have encountered difficulties. Pricing can be prepared for either an entire proposal or for specific options within the proposal. For most sponsors, flexibility is the key.

The most important step in pricing is making an accurate valuation. Therefore, the pricing methods presented in Chapter 6 are critical. Each potential sponsor is engaged in other marketing activities, each of which has a price and value. The sport manager must study and prepare data that demonstrate and accurately translate the benefits of sport sponsorship in terms the corporation can understand. As noted in Chapter 6, it is also important to remember that industry experts estimate an incremental commitment on the part of the sponsor in order to integrate the sponsorship with their existing marketing functions. These can range from an additional 100 to 500% of the sponsorship cost.

Many managers have found one aspect of sport sponsorship difficult to foresee: often, corporations would rather deal with large projects than be victimized by a multitude of small ones (see Fewer, Bigger, Better in Chapter 1). Many sponsorship executives believe that high dollar deals are more profitable and less work that numerous small ventures. Therefore, it is important to offer the company several options in their sponsorship agreement, ranging from exclusive ownership of all events and opportunities to smaller and less expensive options such as value-in-kind (VIK) provisions or associated advertising.

Preparation of the Proposal

There has been some debate regarding the actual appearance of the sponsorship proposal. Some practitioners believe that a quality proposal should have the logo of the sport entity and the sponsor's logo prominently displayed on the cover of the proposal. However, others have cautioned that sponsors may react negatively if their corporate logo was used without permission and question the ethical behavior of the organization. No clear-cut model exists, but a conservative approach would support a professionally prepared proposal without the sponsor's logo. If you are able to arrange a pre-proposal meeting, permission to use their logo may be secured. Another issue arises in the quality of the printing used for the proposal materials. Some authorities have suggested that organizations should prepare the highest quality materials that they can afford. This would include five-color, glossy brochures detailing all of the benefits. On the other hand, some sport marketers believe that the material should be of a more moderate quality to leave the impression that the organization is not frivolous in its spending. The author supports producing the highest quality possible and securing VIK when available to obtain the materials.

The model presented above and the examples shown at the end of the chapter have been derived from existing sponsorship proposals and agreements, and they can provide sport marketers with the skills necessary to succeed in the exciting world of sponsorship.

HONDA CENTER PARTNERSHIP OPPORTUNITIES
(Excerpts Depicting Selected Sponsorship Plan Elements)

EVENT MANAGEMENT

In 2008, the Honda Center ranked second in the country and third in the world in gross ticket sales behind only London's new 02 Arena and New York's Madison Square Garden. Rounding out the top five were Sydney, Australia's Acer Arena and the Thomas and Mack Center in Las Vegas.

IMAGE

Honda Center stands as one of the premier entertainment and sports venues in the country by annually welcoming an average of 1.7 million guests. The Honda Center has welcomed 144 total events, including 33 concerts, since its opening in 1993.

SIGNAGE/EXPOSURE

The 57 Freeway Marquee adds state-of-the-art visibility for Honda Center to the 64 million cars that are seen annually, and it recognizes every partner on its marquee through highly visible, backlit ad panels. The 25-by-27-foot digital LED screen displays rotating messages about upcoming events, as well.

Katella Marquee-The East Katella marquee provides up-to-date information about all Honda Center events. The marquee has quality branding opportunities available on the four backlit panels. There are two panels on each side of the marquee providing visibility to both east-bound and west-bound travelers 24-hours a day.

Scoreboard Signage- The Honda Vision scoreboard provides quality branding opportunities through the following signage elements:

—Four (4) upper panels
—Four (4) lower panels

In-Bowl Signage

—Four (4) corner panels
—Four (4) center scoreboard panels

LED Signage

- Two (2) 360-degree LED rings offer fully-animated, high impact branding opportunities through logo, graphics, and feature presentations
- Exclusive LED visibility during Ducks' games

All-Arena LED partners will receive four (4) minutes of 360-degree LED visibility during the ingress and egress of all non-hockey Honda Center events.

The following are recently created opportunities that give exposure to millions of guests year round,

- Center, East, and West Honda-vision screen
- Naming rights of club level
- Outer walls of club level
- East and West backlit panels
- East and West scrolling ad panel units

Additional signage opportunities include,

- LED ring under Honda-vision
- North and South scrolling panel ad units

HOCKEY SIGNAGE

Dasherboards

- Corner dasherboards
- End-Zone dasherboards
- Mid-Zone dasherboards
- Neutral-Zone dasherboards

Team bench and penalty box

- Signage behind Ducks bench and away team penalty box
- Signage behind away team bench and Ducks penalty box

Player Tunnels

- One (1) sign above Ducks player tunnel
- One (1) sign above away team player tunnel

Zamboni machine tunnel

Zamboni machine wrap

- Branding representation on Zamboni machines utilizing a full wrap
- Two (2) total Zamboni machines on the ice at once
- Visibility to all fans during pre- and post-game and two intermissions

INTEGRATED COMMUNICATIONS

- Placement of sponsor's branded logo on the hondacenter.com website
- High visibility to all website visitors throughout the year
- Creation of customized sponsor web pages and content
- Logo inclusion on more than 175 integrated customizable screens, including 50 HD screens, which will specifically target patrons to help increase brand awareness
- Branding opportunities exist by utilizing 30-second commercial units, as well as static branding messages, bordering the screens of each television in the arena. Screens are located throughout the Plaza level concourse, club level, and all suites.

DUCKS MEDIA

Television Exposure for the 2007/2008 Season

—41 games on FSN and PrimeTicket
—14 games on KDOC
—23 games on FSN West
—4 games on Versus

Television Elements on select broadcasts

—In-game features
—30-second ad spots
—Opening/closing billboards

Radio Elements

—AM 830 will be the flagship station for all 82 Ducks games
—In-game feature
—30 and 60-second in-game spots
—30 and 60-second pre- and post-game spots
—Opening and closing billboards

Media Shows

Sponsorship opportunities for both The Element and DucksTV exist in title sponsorship, ad spots, broadcast features, and other elements that can be mutually developed.

The Element, the official magazine show of Honda Center, is broadcast over-the-air to more than 6 million viewers in Los Angeles and Orange County areas. The show consists of four segments with two to three minute commercial breaks.

DucksTV

* DucksTV is the first ever pre-produced webcast in the NHL. Last year 54 shows were shown with an average monthly viewing of 14,000.

HONDA CENTER ATTENDEE DEMOGRAPHICS

Gender
51% male viewers
49% female viewers

Age
39% adults ages 18 to 24
61% adults ages 35 and older
75% adults ages 18 to 49

HHLD Income
77% of viewers earn $50,000 or more
64% of viewers earn $75,000 or more
46% of viewers earn $100,000 or more

Household
54% of viewers are married
56% of viewers have 1 or more children
70% of viewers own a residence

Education

    72% of viewers have a college degree or above

    14% of viewers have a post-graduate degree

Race

    62% of viewers are White

    27% of viewers are Hispanic

    4% of viewers are Asian

    4% of viewers are Black

    3% of viewers identify with another racial group

HOSPITALITY

- Private, catered suite parties are available in the exclusive Party Suite.
- Season tickets, club tickets, and single game tickets can be purchased.
- Players and team management personnel are available for exclusive dinners and VIP functions.
- Passes to the VIP Blue Line Lounge are provided.
- Sponsorship of in-game promotion during Ducks' games is encouraged. Brand presence can include logo recognition on the LED and Honda Vision, PA announcements, and product displays.

Note: Sincere appreciation is extended to Bob Wagner, senior vice president and chief marketing officer for the Anaheim Ducks, for sharing the above sponsorship package information.

Sponsorship Proposals Worksheets

The worksheets provide a guide for developing various sections of a sponsorship proposal. The following sheets cover the creation of a sponsorship proposal. Complete this worksheet as you would prepare a sponsorship plan.

Provide an overall description of the sponsorship.

_____

_____

_____

_____

_____

_____

_____

_____

_____

_____

Describe the organizing committee and/or management attributes of your staff.

_____

_____

_____
_____
_____

Present the similarities of demographic profiles between the sponsor's customers and your event or property.

_____
_____
_____
_____
_____
_____
_____
_____

Detail the match in psychographic characteristics between the sponsor's customers and your event or property.

_____
_____
_____
_____
_____

Project the anticipated or evaluate the previous media coverage.

_____
_____
_____
_____
_____

List the activities included in the proposal that are designed to enhance sponsor awareness.

_____
_____
_____
_____
_____

List the opportunities included in the proposal that are designed for image building.

_____
_____

_____
_____
_____
_____

Specify elements in the proposal designed to drive sales of sponsor products and services.

_____
_____
_____
_____
_____

Determine the potential for retailer and/or wholesaler tie-ins.

_____
_____
_____
_____
_____

Describe the sponsorship events for developing hospitality relationships.

_____
_____
_____
_____
_____

Examine aspects of the sponsorship that could be used for employee motivation.

_____
_____
_____
_____
_____

Enumerate each of the sponsorable components within the proposal.

_____
_____
_____
_____
_____

_____
_____
_____
_____
_____
_____
_____
_____
_____
_____
_____

Calculate the price of the entire sponsorship for each component in the proposal.

_____
_____
_____
_____
_____
_____
_____
_____
_____
_____
_____

Identify each of the other current sponsors.

_____
_____
_____
_____
_____

Delineate possible risks and your organization's plan to minimize those risks.

_____
_____
_____
_____
_____

Chapter Eight

SECURING SPONSORSHIP AGREEMENTS

Introduction

One of the most difficult decisions you will face after the development of your sponsorship plan will be determining a contact for a particular company. In the industry, this is referred to as the Access or Point of Entry. There has been considerable confusion over the most successful approach to sponsorship acquisition. Recent research ("IEG Survey : Cold call rules," 2007, p. 1) indicates that sponsorships are most often secured through the following entry channels:

55%...... The property approaches the sponsor, known as a cold call.

19%...... The property hires an agency who approaches the sponsor.

13%...... The sponsor contacts the property directly.

8%...... The property board member contacts the sponsor.

5%...... Other entry channels are used.

It is surprising to see the high percentage of the sponsorships that were secured through a "cold call." Cold calls result either from an actual telephone call to the sponsor's organization or from providing an unsolicited proposal through the mail. One of the biggest shock waves through the industry occurred when the $750 million Nextel-NASCAR deal started through a cold call. According to Migala (2003), for anyone selling sports sponsorships, cold calling is easily one of the most dreaded aspects of the job. Migala's advice is that, before you call, you should relax and take 30 seconds to think about what you want to get across. The consensus of the sponsorship buyers he interviewed was that most sellers do not take even a few minutes to think and prepare for a few of the situations that might be waiting on the other end of the line. It is important to have a real sense of why this property is a good fit beyond the obvious reasons. One executive said, "If you are going to make the call, then be prepared. I often get people that say they thought they were going to get voicemail and weren't prepared to have a live conversation. That's no way to start a relationship." Universally, the best beginning to any live conversation is to simply ask the person if it is a good time to talk (Migala, 2003, ¶4).

Voicemail is a way of life. Therefore, voice messages are an important part of the way we communicate. Below is an example of a message that one industry executive thought was ineffective. "Good morning (name), I am sorry to bother you. I know it is a crazy time for you as always, but I want to introduce myself to you over the phone when you have a few minutes. I work for a minor league baseball team in Florida, and even though my research of your marketing activities may or may not lead to a sponsorship immediately, I know that we may meet each other in the future and I would like to start a dialogue when you have time" (Migala, 2003, ¶5). Sponsors would consider this message to be *ineffective*.

Migala (2007, ¶4) presented the top reasons cited by sponsors for not returning a call:

1. The message was all about the property not the brand.

2. The caller was not confident.

3. The caller mentions a competing brand—that alone is enough to delete the message.

4. The caller does not detail the next steps (for example, "I'll call you back on . . .," or "I'll send additional information.").

5. The caller does not leave a return phone number.

6. The caller phones from their cell phone, a no-no on the first call.

All corporations handle sponsorship solicitation differently because the volume of calls is tremendous. Some corporations get as many as 3,000 proposals per year (Seaver, 2004). Recently, many corporations have moved to web-based proposal submission procedures. General Motors has been using an electronic submission process since 1999. Through their in-house marketing agency GM*R Works, they require applicants to complete forms that detail pertinent information about the sponsorship opportunity. Miller Brewing Company also uses an in-house agency but adds a corporate software filter for their proposals.

Some have a localized decision network where the distributor in the area has the authority to make decisions related to sponsorship. In other cases, all sponsorship decisions must be approved at the corporate headquarters. One executive who was seeking a sponsorship deal, and who had extensive experience in working with soft drink and beer sponsors, approached a camera company in the same manner. He knew that the soft drink and beer companies would not consider a sponsorship unless there was a considerable amount of support from local retailers and regional distributors. Unfortunately, after obtaining the backing of field offices for the camera manufacturer, he went to the corporate headquarters only to find that the headquarters didn't like "the tail wagging the dog" (Ukman, 1991, p. 2).

A thorough investigation of the business structure is certainly warranted for each potential sponsor. Coca-Cola, for example, selects 95% of its sponsored events at the local level. So, a sport marketer should not send a proposal to Atlanta without enlisting the support of the local bottler. Both Coke and Pepsi warned high school sport programs that they would not deal with agents or agencies. If the schools were interested in establishing a partnership, they would have to deal directly with the local bottler. Their rationale was simple: they want all of the dollars that go into a deal to benefit the school directly. Their findings had shown that some agents required commissions as high as 40% ("Coke and Pepsi," 1998). A thorough analysis of point-of-access alternatives is becoming more important as corporations are being deluged with requests and many are not accepting unsolicited sponsorship proposals.

Preparing a Cover Letter

Typically after a sport marketer has identified the appropriate point-of-access, one of the first steps is preparing a cover letter. Allen (1998) suggested that a cover letter sent with a sponsorship proposal can often make the difference between getting a sponsorship package read and getting a nice "thanks but no thanks letter." She suggests several trusted rules that should be followed when composing a cover letter (Allen, 1998):

1. Make sure that you send the letter to the proper person at the corporation. Spell his or her name correctly and list the appropriate title. If you don't know this information, call the company switchboard for assistance.

2. Use compelling terminology, as opposed to less effective phrases. Examples of helpful phrases include "measurable response," "reinforce market position," "increase market share," "solidify client relationships," and "integrate marketing opportunities."

3. Make sure that your letter is focused on individually tailored benefits for the recipient. Some of the letter can be from a "template," but the body must be customized for each sponsor with benefits matched to fit the sponsor's needs.

4. Do not make overly general statements that cannot be supported by facts. For example, don't say, "All of the media outlets are excited about this event." Rather, you should indicate which specific media have agreed to cover the event.

5. Do not shift the responsibility of a follow-up to the sponsor (e.g., "I look forward to hearing from you."). Instead, thank the reader for his or her time and indicate that you will call the following week for further discussions regarding the proposal.

Skildum-Reid (2008) notes that too often sponsors who receive proposals are not direct enough with those seeking their support. They typically comment, "Our funds are currently committed," rather than addressing the weakness of the proposal. She believes that a more direct critique of the proposal will ultimately result in properties developing better proposals. For instance, she suggests that the sponsor could say, "We don't consider uncustomized proposals as it shows that you haven't researched our brand and target market needs. Feel free to review our online sponsorship guidelines and resubmit if you feel there is a fit." She provides another possible comment: "It looks like you are really after a philanthropic donation. If we are going to invest marketing funds, we need to see a substantial opportunity to meet marketing and investment objectives."

Sponsorship Proposal Presentations

The following model (Figure 8.1) has been used extensively in many sales situations and seems to work exceptionally well in selling sponsorships. The model begins with establishing your credibility, moves to the identification of challenges, explains how the sponsorship can provide solutions, and concludes with the pricing information.

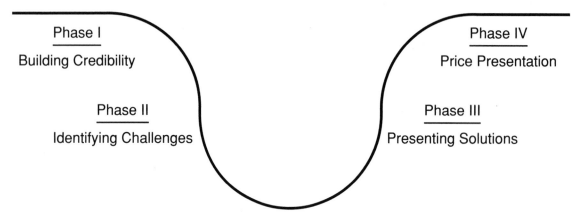

Figure 8.1. Sponsorship Presentation Model

As mentioned in Chapter 3, corporations may be hesitant to allow their image, trademarks, and brands to be managed by an unproven sport organization. Therefore, building credibility (known as Phase I) is essential in securing the corporation's trust. The advertising slogan of the first worldwide Olympic sponsorship program was "a company is judged by the company it keeps." A multitude of factors can lead to the establishment of credibility, including business mannerisms, acceptable protocol, previous performance history, and testimonial evidence. Notwithstanding these factors, personal charm and charisma also contribute to building trust.

Phase II of the process involves an open review of challenges that the potential sponsor may face. The biggest mistake that properties make when presenting proposals to sponsors is focusing too much on what they have to sell; instead, the property should emphasize what the sponsor needs to buy to address their problems. This relates to the marketing theory of product-versus-market orientation. People are more successful selling products and sponsorships that consumers are convinced they need, as opposed to products the salesperson is trying to sell. The challenges sponsors face are often associated with identifying and acquiring customers. The stages of buyer readiness referenced in many marketing texts indicate that buyers move through definable stages in the product adoption process (Pride & Ferrell, 2008). You can demonstrate to sponsors precisely how a sponsorship can address these challenges through the scenarios depicted below.

IDENTIFICATION OF PRODUCT NEED

Example: Consumers may realize they have a need for a particular product if they see that product in use in the sport activity or at the event.

QUEST FOR INFORMATION

Example: Sponsorships can provide information in the form of brochures, program advertisements, product displays, or public address announcements in order to assist consumers with their quest for increased product knowledge.

PRODUCT EVALUATION

Example: Consumers may have information about a company's products but may not have actually tried it. Through product sampling, sponsorships can allow consumers to evaluate the product before deciding to purchase it. If a company has a new product, these activities can motivate consumers toward retail purchase.

PURCHASE OF THE PRODUCT

Example: Many sponsorship packages use coupons as a means to drive sales. These tactics can move in two directions. First, coupons can be made available at the event, or second, sponsors can make discounted ticket coupons available at their retail outlets. Both of these methods have a good history of success. Some success has also been achieved through on-site sales activities.

CUSTOMER SATISFACTION

Example: Most companies gather data on customer satisfaction. Sporting events can provide an excellent backdrop for these activities. You can set up areas for intensive focus group sessions with an array of customer types. This is an activity many sponsors find desirable.

It must be emphasized that the model does not encourage "cross-over" tactics. In other words, you should discuss all of the "challenges" before proceeding to the "solutions" segment (known as Phase III) of the presentation. From a psychological standpoint, this will build momentum for closing the sale. Listening carefully to what the sponsor said during Phase II is critical in presenting the solutions. The following are some concerns frequently expressed by sponsors: "We need to activate our target audience;" "We need a reputable partner;" "Additional media exposure is certainly desirable;" "Can you provide sampling opportunities?" (Stotlar, 2001).

All of these elements were identified as challenges that the NBA could address for Schick Razors through their Official Supplier status. Therefore, the NBA developed extensive product give-away programs at arenas. In the final analysis, Schick's product manager said, "It made sense demographically. The target of men 18 to 34 was a perfect match with NBA audiences" (Schlossberg, 1990, p. 1). Schick also capitalized on their association with the NBA and their target market by sponsoring 700 college Super Hoops tournaments, where the playoffs were conducted at NBA games. Many of Schick's corporate objectives—image enhancement, product trial, and hospitality—tied directly to stages of consumer behavior and were accomplished through their NBA sponsorship.

Closing an agreement and obtaining the payment (known as Phase IV) is typically referred to as "The Ask." Many sport marketers are comfortable making presentations and discussing the virtues of the team or event. However, actually asking someone to hand over a check for $200,000 can be distressing. Negotiating the price of the sponsorship is also a formidable process. As with most business dealings, the physical setting for the negotiation is critical. One approach is to set up a face-to-face meeting, and host it if possible, in order to create an opportunity to demonstrate hospitality. As a side note, don't pull a Coke out from the refrigerator during your meeting with Pepsi executives.

When the Phoenix Coyotes of the NHL scheduled a meeting with Bar S Foods to present sponsorship ideas for the coming season, they proceeded through all of the basic points and then invited the Bar S Foods executives into the front office. There the executives found about 90% of the Coyotes staff having a barbeque lunch, complete with Bar S hotdogs. The Bar S people commented, "Those types of personal touches mean so much, and it has us leaving on such a high note" ("Presenting sponsor," 2004). Hosting the meeting will also allow you to control the timing more effectively. Occasionally, when you have a meeting scheduled at the sponsor's place of business, key executives may be delayed and end up usurping your time allotment.

During the presentation, avoid using any media that involve turning off the lights. It is important to watch the reactions of the audience during the presentation. Therefore, charts, graphs, and portfolios are usually better than Power Point slides or overheads. Computer-generated presentations can be excellent if they do not require the lights to be lowered. Remember, sometimes a marketer has to spend a bit of money on the presentation to make it effective. The owner of the NBA Denver Nuggets and NHL Colorado Avalanche spent $50,000 on the presentation to Pepsi for title sponsorship of the Pepsi Center in Denver. Although the cost was substantial, the presentation was successful.

Negotiations

Negotiations must start with an offer, and because you are the one presenting the proposal, making the offer is always your responsibility. If you have done your homework on pricing, the sponsorship should be valued correctly. However, most business executives will issue a counteroffer. First and foremost, you should acknowledge their willingness to work with you as a sponsor. Next, review the benefits and price-value relationship previously presented—this is a strategy that has met with a lot of success. This often has the effect of reinforcing the message and can result in an agreement. If, however, they continue to suggest a price lower than the asking price, you should reduce the sponsorship package and eliminate some of the associated benefits; in essence, offering them a diminished package (Grey & Skildum-Reid, 2007). Another option would be to offer to locate a co-sponsor to share the costs. At times, it is difficult to walk away from an offer. In 2002, the Arizona Diamondbacks in MLB were coming off of a World Series Championship. They made a presentation to a sponsor priced at $1 million, and the sponsor offered $600,000. They had clearly presented more than $1 million in value and had other sponsors involved at that level. As a result, they had to walk away from the deal. One of the primary reasons for rejecting the offer was to protect the integrity of their other partnerships (Brubaker, 2003). Ultimately, if a sponsor remains steadfast with their first offer after you have reviewed the value and offered to find co-sponsors, then the meeting should be adjourned as the chances are marginal that an agreement will ever result. If the negotiations are successful and an agreement is reached, then your next step is to establish a timeline for contact finalization.

Industry veteran Ethan Green (2004) provided several useful tips for the negotiation process from the sponsor's standpoint. He suggests that sponsors negotiate an exit clause because there are times when situations within the sponsoring company change or the sponsorship fails to deliver on its promised impact. Another clause that should be included is a performance clause. This would tie the sponsorship fee to the claims made by the organization in terms of event attendance, television ratings, or other aspects of the agreement. Such clauses could set a window or conditions under which cancellation would be acceptable or specify the appropriate fees to be reduced. Some sponsorships are directly tied to sales. For example, Gatorade signed a deal with Virginia Beach Parks and Recreation Department in which Gatorade did not pay an up-front fee but based their fee on product sales. They provided $6,000 for the first 1,600 cases of Gatorade sold, $3,000 for the next 1,600, and $1,000 for every additional 1,600 cases sold. The entire sponsorship fee amounted to $15,000 over three years. Green also recommended that sponsors consider including exclusive items in the sponsorship package (also noted in Chapter 7). Sport organizations often have access to game-worn jerseys, autographed merchandise, or other unique items that are not readily available to the general public—sponsors could make valuable use of these items with their clients or employees.

Managing Sponsor Relationships

Managing any business relationship is predicated on the contract existing between the two parties. Sponsorship contracts are critical because many of the terms and concepts remain imprecise. Reed (1990) outlined basic rationale for having a contract:

1. Contracts are needed to clarify the rights assigned to the sponsor and specify the rights retained by the sport organization. Problems have sometimes occurred when sponsors attempted to assign some of their rights to another party. Specifically, during the 2007 NASCAR racing season, Cingular, a cell phone company, was bought out by AT&T. As a result, AT&T desired to replace the Cingular logo on the racecar with its own logo. NASCAR series title sponsor Nextel, a cell phone company with category exclusivity obtained after Cingular's deal, challenged the request. Afterward, a thorough review of contract litigation resulted. An out-of-court settlement allowed the use of the AT&T logo on the car through the 2008 season. Ironically, Nextel was subsequently purchased by Sprint—a warning to always get a contract.

2. The contract should clearly define Title Sponsor, Official Supplier, Presenting Sponsor, and other terms used in the relationship. These terms have no universal meaning or legal interpretation other than what is delineated in the contract.

3. A thorough contract will stipulate the size and placement of all event and stadium signage. Detailed descriptions must be included describing the exact location and dimensions of all signage and assigning the responsibility for manufacturing and erecting the signs.

4. Category exclusivity was noted in Chapter 3 as an important benefit. However, the boundaries of sponsor categories are unclear. For instance, does "financial services" cover banks and credit cards? Does it cover investment services? Therefore, considerable attention must be given to setting category parameters.

5. Contracts are also essential in clarifying the attendant liability of all parties involved. In most instances, sponsors will require that the sport entity include them as a co-insurer on all insurance documents. Sponsors will not risk their corporate assets by exposing them through your own failures, crises, or mismanagement.

6. Protecting the event as an intellectual property is another reason for executing a contract. Several years ago, Coors Brewing Company served as Title Sponsor of the Coors Light Silver Bullet Biathlon Series. However, when it came time for renewal after two successful years of the event, Coors delivered a letter to the originators of the event that stated, "While Coors will evaluate your proposal for possible use in the future, it cannot make any commitments until all programs have been reviewed. . . . Please be advised that Coors may be developing similar or related projects, independent of any promotional ideas, or proposals [XYZ] has submitted" (Stotlar, 2001, p. 119).

   A few weeks later, the organizer received notice that Coors would not be renewing its contract and had, in fact, hired one of the previous organizer's employees to stage an almost identical event for Coors. These types of actions can be reduced through a clause in the contract that restricts the sponsor from staging a similar event for a specified number of years. This is typically called a "covenant not to compete."

7. Contracts are also useful in establishing future rights as a sponsor. Because, in many instance, the full value of sponsorship is not realized in a single year, many sponsors would like to secure the opportunity to retain their sponsorship status. This has been termed the "right of first refusal." This clause mandates that you offer future options to existing sponsors before allowing competitors to sign-on. In 2006, an interesting turn of events happened with MasterCard's longtime sponsorship of the FIFA World Cup; nearing the end of its sponsorship contract, FIFA officials began secret negotiations with MasterCard's rival VISA and announced that they had signed VISA as a new World Cup sponsor. MasterCard immediately sued citing its "right of first refusal" in the existing contract. The courts ultimately agreed with MasterCard and ordered FIFA to accept the negotiated deal with MasterCard. Within a few days of the ruling, four executives were terminated by FIFA. The "right of first refusal" does not restrict you from changing prices from year to year, but it does provide the sponsor with the capacity to continue if their objectives are achieved. To extend benefits from sponsor relationships, most sponsors prefer to sign multi-year contracts covering three to five years and to obtain a "right of first refusal."

Because sport sponsorship represents a partnership, protecting a sponsor's domain is in the sport marketer's best interest. Attending to these contractual details promotes mutual understanding prior to the implementation of a sponsorship alliance. Hopefully, such a relationship will serve the mutual needs of both parties and provide the desired benefits.

Sponsorship Activation Worksheets

The worksheets provide a guide for developing various sections of a sponsorship plan. The following sheets cover the activation of the sponsorship. Complete this worksheet as you would prepare a sponsorship plan.

Draft a cover letter to the person responsible for sponsorship decisions at the sponsor's headquarters.

_____
_____
_____
_____
_____
_____
_____
_____
_____
_____
_____
_____
_____
_____
_____
_____
_____
_____

Develop an outline for your sponsorship proposal presentation.

_____
_____
_____
_____
_____
_____
_____
_____
_____
_____
_____

Structure your negotiation strategies covering possible challenges from the sponsor.

_____
_____
_____

_____

_____

_____

_____

_____

_____

Delineate all administrative tasks for managing the sponsorship.

_____

_____

_____

_____

_____

_____

_____

_____

_____

Chapter Nine

MANAGING SPORT SPONSORSHIPS

Introduction

The sport organization, as the recipient of the sponsorship dollars, has the responsibility of demonstrating the value received by the sponsor. First of all, Spoelstra (1997) suggested, "Do whatever it takes to make the sponsorship successful" (p. 173). In his interviews and research with leading sponsors, Stotlar (1999) found several sponsors who reported that very few sport organizations followed up their partnership with either final reports or supporting data. The sponsorship manager for a major national banking firm indicated that in her 10 years of sponsorship management, only a handful of event managers had submitted reports to her with supporting data. In contrast to this practice, most sponsors now require that fulfillment reports be provided that demonstrate the company's return on the sponsorship investment (Spoelstra, 1997; Stotlar, 1999).

Creating a Sponsorship Report

Spoelstra (1997) suggested that an annual sponsorship report detailing the tangible benefits should be delivered to each sponsor. In its sponsorship contracts, General Motors requires "proof of performance" reports and fulfillment audits before final sponsorship payments are made. In this digital age, the Durham Bulls were one of the first organizations to create their fulfillment report on CD-Rom, therein giving sponsors a great opportunity to see, hear, and experience what they got in return for their partnership with the team. One size does not fit all. Just like your sponsorship proposal, the fulfillment report needs to be customized for each sponsor. In line with this practice, the San Jose Sharks in the NHL are but one of the many professional teams that create a customized report for each sponsor detailing their involvement with the team.

Spoelstra also indicated that best practice would include samples of all sponsorship materials or photos of sponsor images and signage in a "digital scrap book" format for graphic impression. Furthermore, the report should relate all of the promotional activities that the team conducted to support the sponsorship. Not only would this make the company liaison feel secure in their sponsorship decision, but it would also provide them with material to justify their actions within the sponsoring corporation. Amshay and Brian (1998) suggest that sponsors are increasingly demanding a more sophisticated measurement of value. These measures typically parallel those used to evaluate all corporate marketing elements. As Spoelstra remarked, "Prove it to the decision-makers' boss" (p. 172).

The measurement problem exists because, although sponsors want to know the exact return on their investment, sponsorship is difficult to measure. We have mistakenly applied standard advertising metrics to sponsorship measurement: although some of the measures are appropriate, others fail to capture the essence of sponsorship value in generating effective results in the minds and hearts of the consumers (Ukman, 2004).

Measuring Return on Investment (ROI)

Although many corporate officers use ROI measurements to guide all of their business decisions, the rigidity of this approach leaves little room for flexibility. Sponsorship is not as easily quantified as some other business activities. There are certainly quantitative measures that can be employed, but qualitative measures also have their place.

From a quantitative standpoint, many event managers collect data on awareness and recall of sponsor's signage. Several examples of this type of data exist. For example, Turco (1996) conducted research on college basketball fans noting that more than 50% of fans were able to recognize a sponsor's arena signage. Barros, Barros, Santos, and Chadwick (2007) found recognition rates of up to 70% at the Euro 2004 soccer tournament in Portugal. Pitts' investigation of sponsor recognition at the Gay Games IV (1998) indicated that participants were highly cognizant of sponsor identity. Her findings demonstrated that over 75% of participants were able to correctly name three of the four major sponsors with 57.8% identifying the other. This research protocol has also been applied to the elusive Gen Y population. Bennett, Henson, and Zhang (2002) noted that participants and attendees at action sports events, such as the Gravity Games, were able to recognize the sponsors at an impressive 90% rate. These data would be critically important to sponsors, and it is incumbent for sport managers to collect these types of data and report them to corporate partners.

Occasionally, however, problems can occur. What if data showed that no one saw the stadium signage? What if they couldn't remember it after they left the stadium? Exactly this scenario occurred in Stotlar and Johnson's (1989) early research on stadium signage. At one institution, not a single fan surveyed could accurately remember one sign that appeared on the scoreboard. Should the sport organization tell the business that purchased it? First reactions may be to avoid communicating this fact to the sponsor, yet good business practices should mandate it. In the long run, honesty and ethics must prevail. In reality, the sport organization may not know the specific reasons for the company's purchase. The company may have felt some affiliation with the university and would stay on as sponsor anyway. There may also be a need to review decisions regarding the colors and graphics that can affect the fans' response.

It is also important that the consumers are able to recall the name of the sponsor, whether that recollection was spurred by signage, and if recall can be linked to purchasing activities and positive consumer behavior. Data from the 2002 Winter

Olympic Games showed that 72% of people surveyed were able to recognize VISA as an Olympic sponsor. After the 2002 Winter Olympics, 20% of people who recognized VISA as an Olympic sponsor said that they used the credit card company more than the previous month. From its beginning as an Olympic sponsor, VISA's measure of consumer preference as "best overall card" has risen 50%. Their rank as "most accepted card" has doubled. Given that the credit card industry generates over $1 trillion per year in U.S. consumer spending and more than $3 trillion worldwide, these increases in use preference would provide a substantial return on their investment ("VISA USA," 2004; International Olympic Committee, 2002a; International Olympic Committee, 2002b).

Notwithstanding the success of VISA, Stotlar's research (1993) showed that, in general, few people could identify Olympic Sponsors. Most Olympic TOP sponsors had recognition rates of less than 20%. Only two sponsors were able to surpass 50% in consumer recognition as a sponsor. Although the data may look dismal, we cannot jump to the conclusion that spectator recognition was the only—or even primary—motivation of the sponsor.

Skildum-Reid (2007) noted that, although sponsor recall has been a popular metric for measuring success, the end result is to influence consumers, not to see if they can remember a sign that may ultimately have little effect on their purchasing decisions. Olympic sponsors have reported hospitality as a leading objective in providing company executives with an opportunity to interact with their best clients. In any case, additional research would be warranted.

Seaver (2004) noted that a better term for this assessment is "return on objective" (ROO) as opposed to "return on investment." The principle supporting this approach is that a specified value can be placed on attaining a specific objective. Sport marketers could then assess the accomplishment of the objective. For example, in a business-to-business objective to create more favorable opinions about a brand, the sponsor may include hospitality activities at an event. The objective measure, as employed by UPS and their NASCAR sponsorship, would be to track the shipping activities of the attendees against last year's volume. On the other hand, LG Electronics may be more interested in the perceptions of action sports participants who think that LG is a "cool" brand. Qualitative interviews with event participants would reveal the answer. The hope of LG is that eventually the "cool" factor would translate to increased sales. In the Best Practice section of this chapter, there is an example of LG's breakout of the ROO from an action sports event where they hope the "cool brand" image will be further enhanced. Similarly, some corporations that sponsor racing hope that the excitement of racing will transfer to their otherwise unexciting product—a task that is difficult to quantify. In experience marketing, companies want to create "touch points" with their customers. Qualitative research, including interviews and focus groups, is best used to measure these objectives.

Ukman (2004) outlined a basic process for collecting and reporting data to sponsors. She identified the first step in the process as setting objectives and baselines: "Articulating measurable objectives is a prerequisite of effective sponsorship measurement" (Ukman, 2004, p. 3). The objectives should be directional, time-framed, and audience specific. The second step in the process is creating the measurement plan. What types of data are needed to measure the above-stated objectives? Who will be responsible for collecting the data? These issues need to be clarified from the beginning of the sponsorship process. Benchmarks need to be established against which the data can be compared. If a 5% increase in sales is desired, sponsors must know the baseline in order to complete the analysis with post-event data. Data can be collected for multiple sources, such as employees, distributors, spectators, participants, vendors, or the general public. Unfortunately, 86% of sponsors do not spend anything—or spend less than 1%—of their sponsorship budget on measurement. Ukman's third step is implementation of the measurement plan. For example, if the measurement plan was to assess awareness, data, on recall and recognition would be collected. However, if the objectives were to evaluate brand loyalty, then data would need to be collected through audience surveys. Questions like, "Would they recommend this brand to friends?" or "How likely would they be to use this brand?" would be appropriate. Finally, the fourth step in the process is to calculate the return on sponsorship. This includes assigning values to the measurement points in the plan. IEG, Sponsoraid, and other corporations frequently provide benchmark data on the value of sponsorship elements. These are best when applied to discrete markets, as is the case with Sponsoraid, but can also be provided on a national basis, like with IEG.

Sponsor Integration

To ensure the success of sponsorship partners, the sport marketer should assist sponsors with fully integrating their sponsorship activities within their company. Of primary concern is the understanding of the sponsorship rationale by company employees, not just the marketing staff but all of the employees. Educating company employees by clarifying the objectives and the resulting benefits can enhance employee support for and involvement in sponsorship activities ("Five Key Factors," 2004).

Why Sponsors Drop Out

Sponsors cannot be counted on for an indefinite period, as they often drop out for a variety of reasons. Sawyer (1998) identified some of the reasons that sponsors cited for withdrawing from their arrangements. Several sponsors mentioned a decrease in the market value of the event. This was determined either by reduced attendance at a particular event or by a drop in television ratings. When the Women's United Soccer Association (WUSA) folded in 2003, they blamed their demise on lack of sponsorship. The reality was that the WUSA was pricing sponsorship beyond what could be expected in return for value. They were attempting to secure four major sponsors at $10 million each. A review of the opportunities did not show value anywhere near $10 million. Some proposed that this was due to a bias against females, but a closer look suggests that it was actually due to an overpriced product in a market full of competitors. It also reinforces the notion that the WUSA was more interested in what they had to sell as opposed to what the sponsors might want to buy.

On occasion, the cost of sponsoring an event simply prohibits the company. One illustration of this phenomenon was in tennis with sponsorship of the US Open: "So intertwined was Lipton with the event over the last 13 years that it has become known simply as 'The Lipton'" (Kaplan, 1998, p. 15). In many ways, the popularity of the event, and tennis in general, priced Lipton out of title sponsorship. Lipton was no longer able to afford title sponsorship of the event, which totaled $5 million. Furthermore, after eight years of sponsorship with the Open, Pepsi dropped out. A Pepsi executive noted, "The Open is a great hospitality vehicle, but the decision was based on us wanting to concentrate on sports properties that can do more as far as moving cases of soda" (Lefton, 2003, p. 12).

Another regularly cited explanation is a change in corporate direction (Grey & Sklidum-Reid, 2007). In other words, the company had decided that sport sponsorships were no longer in their best interests. One example of this factor was seen in Kodak's departure as an Olympic sponsor. Kodak's chief business officer said, "We loved the Olympics, but unfortunately, the sponsorship only comes once every two years ("Kodak refocuses," 2008). Kodak moved into a multi-year partnership with Six Flags theme park. Similarly, Chinese computer manufacturer Lenovo dropped its sponsorship of the Olympics after Beijing 2008 because "the company will focus more on event sponsorship in strategically targeted markets" (Bloom, 2007, ¶3). Interestingly, Taiwanese computer-maker Acer signed up as a replacement only days after Lenovo's announcement not to renew.

Timing and scheduling during any year is an aspect that the sport manager may have little control over. Events and opportunities may come in conflict with other corporate advertising or sponsorship campaigns. This reason alone has left many sport organizers without sponsorship even though their data and proposals were attractive. Sawyer (1998) also found that, although multiple factors and hard data were required to convince a sponsor to initiate a sponsorship, one negative attribute was sufficient to cause a sponsor to drop out.

Preventing Dropout

Ukman (2003) stated the obvious when she said, "Too many sponsorship program[s] are dropped, not because they don't have measurable value, but because the value was not measured" (p. 2). Giving service to sponsors can prevent dropout. Simply stated, "under-serviced (or worse yet, un-serviced) sponsors leave" (Skildum-Reid, 2008, p. 9). As noted previously, Joyce Julius & Associates has, as its main business, the provision of the type of data that can demonstrate a sponsorship value. Its analysis of sporting event television coverage provides estimates of the advertising value of the corporate logo's appearance and the announcers' product and corporate mentions in relation to the time of on-screen presence. Supporting information should also be collected and provided by the sport organization. Factors such as attendance and crowd demographics are of particular importance to sponsors and are almost always readily available. Additional information on the psychographics, buying habits, attitudes, and loyalty of attendees is also critical for sponsors. The more you know about your event and its audience, the more power you will have in attracting and keeping sponsors.

As has been suggested, data needed to justify involvement in sport sponsorships are important to both the event owner and the sponsor. The best practice is to complete an accurate and extensive post-event report that details the value of the sponsorship. As a final note, if you don't provide this information, the company executive who signed the $300,000 sponsorship check may not still be employed when renewal comes around. And they certainly won't be happy with a cancelled check as the only feedback on their investment. Hopefully, by following the guidelines and recommendations presented throughout this workbook, you will be successful in developing and implementing successful sport sponsorship plans of your own.

Best Practice

LG Electronics, a large Korean-based company known mostly for its cell phones that also produce digital appliances and flat screen televisions, was title sponsor of the 2003 LG Action Sports Championships held in Los Angeles. Below, you will find information ranging from their objectives to the post-event measurement activities. The key points in this case include LG's integration, activation, and measurement practices.

LG ACTION SPORTS CHAMPIONSHIPS

LG Objectives

1. To increase brand awareness and create familiarity between LG and the target audience in action sports and music through pre-event marketing initiatives and on-site activation.

2. To build a compelling interactive experience in order to engage the target audience in a personal and memorable way so that LG's sponsorship will remain with the consumer long after the event is over.

Event Data

Attendance-31,368 attendees, 45% of which fall into the 15 to 17 age group. 73% of attendees had a cell phone and the remainder had a high intent to purchase.

Sales Potential

Potential LG cell phone purchases-25% of attendees, or roughly 8,000 people, will purchase cell phones in the next year. The average price of a phone is $200. 2,640 were either likely or somewhat likely, when phones were discounted 50%, to purchase LG. Therefore, the market sales potential is $528,000.

Key Marketing Elements

Pre-Event Television

75 30-second placements generating 1.2 million impressions valued at $303,400.

Road to the LG Action Sports Championships featuring 399,000 60-minute placements valued at $72,000.

Pre-Event Online

LG "Pic Trick" voting at website and randomly drawn product give-a-ways.

3,796 voters from 4,662 unique visitors valued at $8,400.

On-site Activation

LG Lounge

VIP hospitality

Music stage

LG phone girls

Pic Trick sweepstakes

Enter to win raffle

Athlete appearances

Product demonstration kiosks

"Name That Tone" game

LG cell phone inflatables

Participant gift packs with LG products and logo souvenirs

Management Worksheets

The worksheets provide a guide for developing various sections of a sponsorship plan. The following sheets cover the management of the sponsorship, including the final report to the sponsor. Complete this worksheet as you would prepare a sponsorship plan.

Identify the person responsible for sponsor services.

_____

_____

Complete the Post-Event Report.

List the event date: _____

Report the attendance: _____

Calculate the audience (immediate and mediated numbers).

_____
_____
_____
_____
_____

Report the demographic profile of the audience.

_____
_____
_____
_____

Specify the media coverage and compute the commercial value attained.

_____
_____
_____
_____
_____
_____
_____
_____
_____
_____

Record the impressions/recognition data for all sponsorship elements.

_____
_____
_____
_____
_____
_____
_____
_____
_____

Record the qualitative data for appropriate sponsorship elements.

_____
_____
_____
_____

_____

_____

_____

_____

_____

_____

Prepare the final report for the sponsor (as applicable).

_____

_____

_____

_____

_____

_____

_____

_____

_____

_____

_____

References

12 top companies. (1991, February). *The Magazine of the Organizing Committee of the XVI Winter Games*, 44–45.

A tale of two districts: Texas schools take a different approach to sponsorship (2003). Retrieved November 17, 2003, from http://www.sponsorship.com/iegsr/2003/11/17/2003/4704.asp?

Allen, S. (1998). *Pitching with a pen.* Holmdel, NJ: Allen Consulting, Inc.

Ambush marketing: Under control in Nagano. (1998, Summer). *Olympic Marketing Matters*, 9.

Amis, J., Pant, N., & Slack, T. (1997). Achieving a sustainable competitive advantage: A resource-based view of sport sponsorship. *Journal of Sport Management, 11*(1), 80–95.

Amshay, T., & Brian, V. (1998, July 20–26). Sport sponsorship sword cuts both ways. *SportsBusiness Journal*, 23.

A.R.C. (1998, May). Sponsorship park and roll. *Athletic Business*, 18.

Audi of America named official auto sponsor of US ski team. Retrieved November 30, 2007, from http://sponsorship.com/news/prekentico-aarchives

Bank of America announces US Olympic Team sponsorship through 2008 Olympic Games. (2004). Retrieved May 17, 2004, from http://www.sponsorship.com/News/Content/5411.asp?source=iotw051704

Barros, C. P., Barros, C., Santos, A., & Chadwick, S. (2007). Sponsorship Brand recall at the Euro 2004 soccer tournament. *Sport Marketing Quarterly, 16*(3), 161–170.

Baseball's Cubs run free funeral promotion. (2004). *Stadia*. Retrieved May 21, 2004, from http://www.stadia.tv.archive/user/news_article.tpl?id=20040521160041

Bayor, L. (1996, May 20). Atlanta fends off megasigns. *Advertising Age*, 30.

Bennett, G., Henson, R., & Zhang, J. (2002). Action sports sponsorship recognition. *Sport Marketing Quarterly, 11*(3), 25–34.

Bernstein, A. (1998a, June 22–28). High tech a [virtual] sign of the times. *SportsBusiness Journal, 24*, 36.

Bernstein, A. (1998b, June 22–28). Leagues hit it big in gold rush. *SportsBusiness Journal, 19*, 32.

Bernstein, A. (1998c, September 14–20). Teams scramble for sponsorship. *SportsBusiness Journal, 1*, 5.

Bernstein, A. (1998d, September 29–October 4). Working both sides of the plate. *SportsBusiness Journal, 19*, 28.

Bloom, H. (2007, December 5). That was quick, Lenovo out as Olympic Sponsor. *Sport Business Network Daily Dose*, 3.

Bloom, H. (2008). *The Daily Dose.* Retrieved June 6, 2008, from http://www.sportsbusinessnews.com/

Boyd, T., & Shank, M. (2004). Athletes as product endorsers: The effect of gender and product relatedness. *Sport Marketing Quarterly, 13*(2), 82–93.

Brockington, L. (1998, September 21–27). Isuzu drops tourney sponsorship. *SportsBusiness Journal*, 3.

Brooks, C. M. (2001, Spring). Using sex appeal as a sport promotion strategy. *Women in Sport & Physical Activity Journal, 10*(1), 1–11.

Brooks, C. M., & Harris, K. K. (1998). Celebrity athlete endorsement: An overview of the key theoretical issues. *Sport Marketing Quarterly, 7*(2), 34–44.

Brubaker, S. (2003). Negotiations part one: Executives outline approach to say no to a prospective sponsor. *Team Marketing Report, 15*(4), 7.

Buffalo Bills look to increase signage revenue by creating quadrant sponsorships in Rich Stadium. (1996, June). *Team Marketing Report, 1*, 7.

Carter, L., & Wilkinson, I. (2002, July). *Reasons for sponsoring the Sydney 2000 Olympic Games.* Paper presented at ANZMAC 2000 Visionary Marketing for the 21st Century: Facing the Challenge.

Castiglione, J. (1989, May). Good neighbors. *College Athletic Management*, 31–33.

Chua, Y. (2002, Jul/Aug). China moves to protect Olympic insignia. *Managing Intellectual Property*, 56.

Coke and Pepsi warn schools: No sponsorships via agents (1998, August 31). *IEG Sponsorship Report*, 1–2.

Copeland, R., Frisby, W., & McCarville, R. (1996). Understanding the sport sponsorship from a corporate perspective. *Journal of Sport Management, 10*(1), 32–48.

Cordiner, R. (2002a, June-July). Boxing and sponsorship: A mismatch of a knockout combination. *International Journal of Sports Marketing and Sponsorship*, 175–181.

Cordiner, R. (2002b, January). Sponsors of the wide world of sport—what's in it for them? *Sports Marketing*, 14–16.

Cordova, J. (1996, January). *Coca-Cola's sponsorship objectives.* Paper presented at the National Sports Forum, Colorado Springs, CO.

Currie, N. (2004, March). Interview with Nigel Currie, joint chairman European Sponsorship Association. *International Journal of Sports Marketing and Sponsorship*, 246–251.

Dannon sponsorship stirs 3-to-1 return. (2003). *IEG Sponsorship Report, 22*(21), 1–2.

Danylchuk, K. (1998, November). *Sponsorship of the LPGA du Maurier Classic: Will it go up in smoke?* Paper presented at the Conference of the Sport Management Association of Australia and New Zealand, Gold Coast, Australia.

DeParle, J. (1989, September). Warning: Sports stars may be hazardous to your health. *Washington Monthly*, 34–48.

Drehs, W. (2004). *Winston washed out in sea of yellow and black.* Retrieved February 12, 2004, from http://sports.espn.go.com/rpm/news/story?id=1733753

EA Sports gives teams and sponsors numerous options for video games. (1998, March). *Team Marketing Report*, 6.

Eaton, B. (2004, May 19). *VISA USA strengthens ties with USA Gymnastics through 2008.* Retrieved May 21, 2004, from http://www.sponsorship.com/News/Content/5424.asp?source=iotw052004

Ehrlich, D. (1998, June 1–7). Sponsors target Cup's huge audience. *SportsBusiness Journal*, 26.

Evinrude renews long-term sponsorship of FLW Outdoors (2004). Retrieved July 2, 2004, from http//:www.sponsorship.com/news/content/5610.asp?source=iotw70104

Ferrel, M. (1999, November 22–28). The network advantage. *Sports Business Journal*, 30–31.

Fink, J., Kensicki, L., Fitzgerald, M., & Brett, M. (2004, June). *Using female athletes as endorsers of events: Attractiveness versus expertise*. Paper presented at the Conference of the North American Society for Sport Management, Atlanta, GA..

Finley, B. (1998, December 24). Utah bid probed by feds. *Denver Post*, pp. 1A, 15A.

Five key factors that ensure relevant activation and sponsorship success (2004). *IEG Sponsorship Report, 23*(11), 1–3.

Freedman, J. (2008). *Fortunate 50*. Retrieved June 18, 2008, from http://sportsillustrated.cnn.com/more/specials/fortune50/2008/index.html

Freidman, A. (1999, March-April 4). Rare glimpse at the selling of a stadium. *SportsBusiness Journal*, 36–37.

FTC v. Pinkerton Tobacco Company. (1991, October 28). File No. 9023006. United States Federal Trade Commission.

Fullerton, S. (2007). *Sports marketing*. New York: McGraw-Hill Irwin.

Gatlin, G. (2003, December 31). In endorsements, youth wins. *Boston Herald*, p. O27.

Germany ready to tangle over tobacco ban. (1998, July 20–26). *SportsBusiness Journal*, 21.

Glase, T. (2003, September 18). Serena Williams voted most marketable female athlete. *SportsBusiness Daily, 6*(2), 10.

Goldberg, R. (1998a, June 22–28). Co-branding ideal for sponsors who want to go the extra mile. *SportsBusiness Journal*, 22.

Goldberg, R. (1998b, June 22–28). Toughest task: Measuring results. *SportsBusiness Journal*, 29.

Goldman, L. (2000). Going to xtremes. *Forbes, 165*(8), 18.

Graham, S. (1998, June 22–28). Rights deals making a play for sales value. *SportsBusiness Journal*, 34.

Greater TOP support. (1999, January). *Olympic Marketing Matters*, 10.

Green, E. (2002). *The Compaq Way*. Paper presented at the 2002 National Sports Forum, Boston, MA.

Green, E. (2004). *Ethan Green's ten tips of improve sponsor negotiations*. Retrieved June 6, 2004, from http://www.migalareprot.com/june 04/negotitations.cfm

Greenwald, L., & Fernandez-Balboa, J. M. (1998). Trends in the sport marketing industry and in the demographics of the United States: Their effect on the strategic role of grassroots sport sponsorship in corporate America. *Sport Marketing Quarterly, 7*(4), 35–48.

Grey, A. M., & Skildum-Reid, K. (2007). *Sponsorship seekers toolkit* (2nd ed.). Sydney: McGraw Hill.

Hagstrom, R. (1998). *The NASCAR way*. New York: Wiley.

Hein, K. (2003, July 14). A broken field of dreams. *Brandweek*, 15.

Henderson, J. (2008, June 29). US coach faces suit over suit. *Denver Post*, p. 16C.

Hotzau, A. (2007a, September). Vancouver 2010. *Sport Decision Intelligence Report*, 2–4.

Hotzau, A. (2007b, April). Ambush marketing. *Sport Decision Intelligence Report*, 1–3.

Hugo Boss renews Davis Cup tie through 2012. (2007). Retrieved November 30, 2007, from http://sponsorship.com/news——information/news/pre-kentico-archives

IEG (2003, October 20). IEG survey. *IEG Sponsorship Report, 22*(19), 3–4.

IEG (2007). Mixed bag: Sponsorship spending to surge in '08. *IEG Sponsorship Report, 26*(24), 1, 4–5.

IEG Survey: Cold calls rule. (2007, October 15). *IEG Sponsorship Report, 26*(19), 1, 4–5.

International Olympic Committee (2002a). *Marketing fact file*. Lausanne: International Olympic Committee.

International Olympic Committee (2002b). *Salt Lake 2002 marketing report*. Lausanne: International Olympic Committee.

International Olympic Committee (2004). *Marketing fact file*. Lausanne: International Olympic Committee.

International Olympic Committee. (2006). *International Olympic Committee manufacturer identification guidelines for the 2008 Beijing Olympic Games*. Lausanne: International Olympic Committee.

Irwin, R. L., Assimakopoulos, M. K., & Sutton, W. A. (1994). A model for screening sport sponsorship opportunities. *Journal of Promotion Management, 2*(3/4), 53–69.

Irwin, R. L., & Sutton, W. A. (1994). Sport sponsorship objectives: An analysis of their relative importance for major corporate sponsors. *European Journal of Sport Management, 1*(2), 93–101.

Irwin, R., Lackowitz, T., Cornwell, B., & Clark, J. (2003). Cause-related sport sponsorship: An assessment of spectator beliefs, attitudes and behavioral intentions. *Sport Marketing Quarterly, 12*(3), 131–137.

Isidore, C. (2004a). *Tiger's still a winner for sponsors*. Retrieved June 21, 2004, from http://www.money.cnn.com/2004/06/18/comentary-sports-biz/index.htm

Isidore, C. (2004b). *Big win for the little guys*. Retrieved April 30, 2004, from http://www.money.cnn.com/2004/04/30/comentary/column_sportbiz/index.htm

Jackson, J. (2007, May 6). The rich list. *Observer Sports Magazine*, 56–58.

Johnson, G. (1998, April 21). Kids sports go commercial. *Akron Beacon Journal*, p. C7.

Jones, P. D. (1997, January). Better to give and to receive. *Hemispheres*, 33–38.

Joyce Julius & Associates. (2008). *Second look*. Retrieved March 8, 2008, from http://www.joycejulius.com/newletter/a-second-look-mar-2008.htm

Joyce, M. (2003, June 23–29). Alt-sport execs see growth and growing pains for category's events and sponsors. *SportsBusiness Journal*, 8.

Kaplan, D. (1998a, September 7–13). Lipton to bow out of title sponsorship. *SportsBusiness Journal*, 15.

Kaplan, D. (1998b, September 7–13). Venus patches rift with WTA. *SportsBusiness Journal*, 9.

Kaplan, D. (2007, October 8–14). Upshaw: Apparel fines from NFL 'out of hand.' *SportsBusiness Journal, 10*(19), 5.

Kaplan, D. (2008, June 16–22). EA's contract with NFLPA. *SportsBusiness Journal, 11*(9), 4.

Kaufman, M. (1998, May 11–17). Women take their place at the table. *SportsBusiness Journal, 1*, 48.

Keeping the Olympics' ideal (1997, April). *Sports Business*, 32–33.

Kennet, P. A., Sneath, J. Z., & Erdmann, J. W. (1998, Winter). The quantitative and qualitative benefits of sponsoring the 1996 Olympics: An exploratory study. *International Sports Journal*, 115–126.

King, B. (1998, August 17–23). Earnhardt wants to tune up your engine. *SportsBusiness Journal*, 9.

King, B., & Bernstein, A. (1998, April 27–May 3). Teams lose logo rights in shoe deals. *SportsBusiness Journal, 1*, 53.

Kodak and the Games: A legacy of support. (2004). Retrieved July 19, 2004, from http://sponsorship.com/news/content/5675.asp?source=iotw071904

Kodak refocuses, repurposes role of sponsorship. (2008). Retrieved February 12, 2008, from http://www.sponsorhsip.com/iegsr/subsonly/topic_article.asp?id=5685

Kuzma, J. R., Shanklin, W. L., & McCally, J. F. (1993). Number one principle for sporting events seeking corporate sponsors: Meet benefactor's objectives. *Sport Marketing Quarterly, 2*(3), 27–32.

Landmark settlement restricts tobacco marketers to one brand deal per year. (1998, November 23). *IEG Sponsorship Report*, 1–2.

Lauletta, S. (2003). Negotiations part one: Executives outline approach to say no to a prospective sponsor. *Team Marketing Report, 15*(4), 8.

Lee, J. (2003, September 22–28). College deals build brand and relationships. *SportsBusiness Journal*, 25.

Lefton, T. (2003a, October 6–12). Pepsi out as sponsor of US Open tennis. *SportsBusiness Journal*, 12.

Lefton, T. (2003b, October 27–November 2). Little league touches all the bases with four multiyear sponsorships. *SportsBusiness Journal*, 13.

Liberman, N. (2008, February 18–24). State farm aims at youthful market. *SportsBusiness Journal*, 22.

Lindsay, E. (2008, January 14–20). A futile search. *SportsBusiness Journal, 10*(37), 24.

Lomas, G. (2004). *F1 stars rake in the big bucks.* Retrieved April 13, 2004, from LexisNexis database.

Lombardo, J. (1998a, May 4–10). 'Team Tiger' takes Woods to the top. *SportsBusiness Journal*, 22–23.

Lombardo, J. (1998b, May 18–24). Reebok downsizing NBA deal. *SportsBusiness Journal*, 6.

Lombardo, J. (2004, July 19–25). Nike endorsers will dominate Reebok-clad US hoops team. *SportsBusiness Journal*, 5.

Lombardo, J. (2008). Will shifting NBA courtside signs boost revenues? *SportsBusiness Journal, 11*(8), 1, 54.

Macnow, G. (1989, September). Sports tie-ins help firms score big. *IEG Sponsorship Report*, 1.

Marketing issues. (1997, Summer). *Olympic Marketing Matters*, 2–3.

Marsano, W. (1987, September). A five ring circus. *Northwest*, 64–69.

McCarthy, M. (2003, August 22). Win or lose, drawing endorsements is key. *USA Today*, p. 1B.

McCarville, R., & Copeland, B. (1994). Understanding sport sponsorship through exchange theory. *Journal of Sport Management, 8*(2), 102–114.

McDonald, M. (1998, June). *Sport sponsorship and the role of personality matching.* Paper presented at the Conference of the North American Society for Sport Management, Buffalo, NY.

McKelvey, M. (2003, Winter). Commercial Branding: The final frontier or false start for athletes' use of temporary tattoos as body billboards. *Journal of the Legal Aspects of Sport, 6*(4). Retrieved September 3, 2003, from LexisNexis database.

Michel, A. (1991, October). *Economics of the 1992 Albertville Olympics.* Paper presented at the International Sport Business Conference, Columbia, SC.

Mickle, T. (2008a, January 23–February 3). Translating into an endorsement. *SportsBusiness Journal, 10*(39), 1.

Mickle, T. (2008b, June 16–22). USOC tries to cap swimming deals. *SportsBusiness Journal, 11*(9), 1, 6.

Migala, D. (2003). Turing cold calls into hot leads. *Migala Report.* Retrieved November 4, 2003, from http://www.migalareport.com/nov03_story3.cfm

Migala, D. (2004a). Be a good host: How to increase revenue thought non-traditional hospitality outings. *Migala Report.* Retrieved March 3, 2004, from http://www.migalareport.com/reports.cfm?report=mar04_story2.cfm

Migala, D. (2004b). Presenting sponsor: How to jazz up your sponsorship sales presentation. *Migala Report.* Retrieved January 5, 2004, from http://www.migalareport.com/jan04_story3.cfm

Migala, D. (2004c). What's the buzz: Activation is the buzzword among marketers. *Migala Report.* Retrieved March 3, 2004, from http://www.migalareport.com/reports.cfm?report=mar04_story1.cfm

Migala, D. (2007a). Attention: How to get noticed by a sponsor in a modern sponsorship sales environment. *Migala Report.* Retrieved December 4, 2007, from http://www.migalareport.com/reports.cfm?=dec07_story3.cfm

Migala, D. (2007b). Key to new sponsor revenues. *Migala Report.* Retrieved December 4, 2007, from http://www.migalareport.com/reports.cfm?reports=story4.cfm

Motion, J., Leitch, S., & Brodie, R. (2003). Equity in corporate co-branding. *European Journal of Marketing, 37*(7/8), 1080–1094.

Muellner, A. (1998, August 3–9). Nike ups its investment in Miami community causes. *SportsBusiness Journal*, 8.

Mullen, L. (1998, October 5–11) Biz woes reach golfers. *SportsBusiness Journal*, 3.

Mushett, M. (1995, June). *Sponsorship and the Paralympic Games.* Paper presented at the Conference of the North American Society for Sport Management, Atlanta, GA.

Myerson, A. R. (1996, May 31) Olympic sponsors battling to defend turf. *New York Times*, pp. D1, D17.

Nautica signs apparel sponsorship with US sailing teams. (2004, May 21). Retrieved May 21, 2004, from http://www.sponsorship.com/News/Content/5425.asp?source=iotw052004

Nextel launches exclusive wireless service. (2004). Retrieved June 28, 2004, from http://www.sponsorship.com/news/content/5593.asp?sources+iotw062804

Olympic Fact File. (1998). Lausanne: International Olympic Committee.

Olympic Fact File. (2000). Lausanne: International Olympic Committee.

Olympic Fact File. (2004). Lausanne: International Olympic Committee.

Pepsi wants bigger number of smaller multicultural properties. (May 3, 2004). *IEG Sponsorship Report, 23*(8), 1–3.

Performance Research. (2004). *Sponsorship spending and decision making.* Retrieved March 3, 2004, from http://www.performanceresearch.com/sponsorship-spending.htm

Pitoniak, S. (2008). Lorean Ochoa a winner on and off course. Retrieved June 18, 2008, from http://www.lorenaochoa.com/noticias_ing.html

Pitts, B. G. (1998). An analysis of sponsorship recall during Gay Games IV. *Sport Marketing Quarterly, 7*(4), 11–18.

Pitts, B. G. (2003, October). *Banking on the pink dollar: Sponsorship and the Gay Games.* Paper presented at the Sport Marketing Association Annual Conference, Gainesville, FL.

Pollack, J. (1996, May 20). Kraft teams up brands for Olympic sponsorship. *Advertising Age*, 30.

Ponturo, T. (2002). *What sponsors want*. Panel discussion at the 2002 National Sports Forum, Pittsburgh, PA.

Poole, M. (2003, October 27–November 2). It's a new sponsorship world and agencies can thrive if they adapt. *SportsBusiness Journal*, 14.

Poole, M. (2007, March-April). Grasping sponsor expectations critical for sport properties. *SportsBusiness Journal*, 16.

Popke, M. (2002, October). Your name here. *Athletic Business*, 42–44.

Pratzmark, R. R., & Frey, N. (1989, January). The winners play a new global game. *Marketing Communications*, 18–27.

Pride, W. M., & Ferrell, O. C. (2008) *Marketing* (14th ed.). New York: Houghton Mifflin Company.

Product integration: Not just for technology companies anymore (2004, May 3). Assertions. *IEG Sponsorship Report, 23*(8), 1, 3.

Reed, M. H. (1990). *Legal aspects of promoting and sponsoring events*. Chicago: International Events Group.

Reynolds, M. (1998, June 22–28). Women's sport: A growth area. *SportsBusiness Journal*, 30.

Ries, A., & Trout, J. (1986). *Positioning: The battle for your mind*. New York: McGraw-Hill.

Rodin, S. (1998, May 11–17). Shrewd marketers can share in boom. *SportsBusiness Journal*, 34.

Rohm, A. (1997). The creation of consumers bonds within running. *Sport Marketing Quarterly, 6*(2), 17–25.

Rovell, D. (1998, September 14–20). Sports video games an untapped market. *SportsBusiness Journal*, 37.

Rovell, D. (2004). *Sports biz*. Retrieved Feb 23, 2004, from http://sports.espn.go.com/espn/sportbusiness/news/story?id=174215

Roy, D., & Graeff, T. (2003). Consumer attitudes toward cause-related marketing activities in professional sport. *Sport Marketing Quarterly, 12*(3), 163–172.

Rozin, S. (1998, February 21). Why corporate support is good business. *Forbes Special Advertising Section*, 42–48.

Salt Lake Organizing Committee. (1998, September 18). *Salt Lake 2002: Basic plan for the XIX Olympic Games*. Salt Lake City: Salt Lake Organizing Committee.

Saunders, S. (1996, January). *Does it sell beer?* Paper presented at the National Sports Forum, Colorado Springs, CO.

Sawyer, L. (1998, January). *Why sponsors drop out*. Paper presented at the National Sports Forum, Boston, MA.

Schlossberg, H. (1990a, April 2). Sports marketing. *Marketing News*, p. 1.

Schlossberg, H. (1990b, April 7). Allure of Celebrity Endorsers Starts to Fade. *Marketing News*, p. 7.

Seaver, R. (1996, January) *Survey of the industry*. San Diego: Seaver Marketing Group.

Seaver, R. (2004). *2004 corporate sponsorship survey report*. San Diego: Seaver Marketing Group.

Shaun White and Burton sign 10 year endorsement deal. (2008). Retrieved June 18, 2008, from http://www.snowboard-mag.com/node/29532

Sherwin-Williams inks partnership with Big South. (2004). Retrieved February 26, 2004, from http://www.sponsorship.com/content/5056.asp?source=iotw022604

Skildum-Reid, K. (2007). *Ambush marketing toolkit*. Sydney: McGraw-Hill.

Skildum-Reid, K. (2008a). *All our funds are currently committed*. Retrieved February 29, 2008, from http://www.powersponsorship.com/blog.aspx#136

Skildum-Reid, K. (2008b). *It's all about you*. Retrieved February 29, 2008, from http://www.powersponsorship.com/blog.aspx#136

Skildum-Reid, K. (2008c). *Image transfer*. Retrieved February 29, 2008, from http://www.powersponsorship.com/blog.aspx#136

Skildum-Reid, K. (2008d). *Pricing based on your need*. Retrieved February 29, 2008, from http://www.powersponsorship.com/blog.aspx#136

Skildum-Reid, K. (2008e). *Return on investment*. Retrieved February 29, 2008, from http://www.powersponsorship.com/blog.aspx#136

Skildum-Reid, K. (2008f). *Technology is a sponsor's best friend*. Retrieved February 29, 2008, from http://www.powersponsorship.com/blog.aspx#136

Skildum-Reid, K. (2008g). *Under-serving*. Retrieved February 29, 2008, from http://www.powersponsorship.com/blog.aspx#136

Smart brand vehicles to lead runners in the 108th Boston Marathon. (2004). Retrieved April 4, 2004, from http://sponsorship.com/news/content/5257.asp?source=iotw041504

Smith, M. (2007, December 3–9). Key revenues and expenses for college bowls. *SportsBusiness Journal, 10*(32), 30–33.

Spiegel, P. (1998, December 14). Heir Gordon. *Forbes*, 188–197.

Spoelstra, J. (1997). *Ice to the Eskimos*. New York: Harper Business.

Sponsors of the Beijing 2008 Olympic Games. (2008). Retrieved September 15, 2008, from http://en.beijing2008.cn/bocog/sponsors/sponsors

Sponsors identify peak-performing properties. (2008, July 14). *IEG Sponsorship Report, 27*(13), 1, 3–4.

Sponsors reveal return on investment. (1997, March 31). *IEG Sponsorship Report*, 5.

Strategic philanthropy: Building social capital and financial returns. (2004). Retrieved June 28, 2004, from http://www.sponsorship.com/sproducts/109_product_agenda.asp

Staying ahead of the Games: Visa banks and merchants post Olympic results. (2004). *IEG Sponsorship Report, 23*(14), 7.

Stone, G., Joseph, M., & Jones, M. (2003). An exploratory study on the use of sport celebrities in advertising: A content analysis. *Sport Marketing Quarterly, 12*(2), 94–102.

Stotlar, D. K. (1993). Sponsorship and the Olympic winter games. *Sport Marketing Quarterly, 2*(3), 35–46.

Stotlar, D. K. (1999). Sponsorship in North America: A survey of sport executives. *Journal of Sport Marketing and Sponsorship, 1*(1), 87–100.

Stotlar, D. K. (1997, June). *Xerox: A case study of Olympic sponsorship*. Paper presented at the Annual Conference of the North American Society for Sport Management, San Antonio, TX.

Stotlar, D. K. (2001). *Developing successful sport marketing plans*. Morgantown, WV: Fitness Information Technology.

Stotlar, D. K. (2005). *Developing successful sport marketing plans* (2nd ed.). Morgantown, WV: Fitness Information Technology.

Stotlar, D. K., & Johnson, D. M. (1989, July). Assessing the impact and effectiveness of stadium advertising on sport spectators at division one institutions. *Journal of Sport Management, 3*(2), 90–102.

Talalay, S. (2008, February 12). New website connects Florida Panther's business partners. *Florida Sun Sentinel*, p. B1.

Thwaites, D., & Aguilar-Manjarrez, R. (1997). *Sport sponsorship de-*

velopment among leading Canadian companies. Montpellier, France: Forth European Congress on Sport Management.

Tomasini, N., & Stotlar, D. (2003, October). Corporate sponsorship differences between Division I-A, I-AA, and I-AAA institutions. Paper presented at the Sport Marketing Association Annual Conference, Gainesville, FL.

TOP IV Programme. (1997, Summer). Olympic Marketing Matters, 8.

Turco, D. M. (1996). The effects of courtside advertising on product recognition and attitude change. Journal of Sport Management, 5(4), 11–15.

Two new partners. (1997, Summer). Olympic Marketing Matters, 9.

Ukman, L. (1991, April 8). Assertions. Special Events Reports, 2.

Ukman, L. (1995). IEG's complete guide to sponsorship. Chicago: International Events Group.

Ukman, L. (1995, December 4). Back to basics. IEG Sponsorship Report, 14(24), 2.

Ukman, L. (1997a, January 17). Assertions. International Events Group. Retrieved January 23, 1997, from http://www.sponsorship.com

Ukman, L. (1997b, August 18). Assertions. IEG Sponsorship Report, 18(19), 2.

Ukman, L. (1998a, March 20). Assertions. IEG Sport Sponsorship Report, 19(5), 2.

Ukman, L. (1998b, October 26). Assertions. IEG Sponsorship Report, 19(20), 2.

Ukman, L. (2003a). Assertions. IEG Sponsorship Report, 22(21), 2.

Ukman, L. (2003b). Assertions. IEG Sponsorship Report, 22(24), 2.

Ukman, L. (2004a). Return on sponsorship. Chicago: International Events Group.

Ukman, L. (2004b, May 3). Assertions. IEG Sponsorship Report, 23(8), 1–3.

Ukman, L. (2004c, May 31). Assertions. IEG Sponsorship Report, 23(10), 2.

Ukman, L. (2008, March 17). Decision maker survey shows confidence in sponsorship. Sponsorship Report, 27(5), 1–3.

United States Olympic Committee. (2002). 2002 annual report. Colorado Springs: United States Olympic Committee.

United States Olympic Committee. (2004). Retrieved July 2, 2004, from http://www.usolympicteam.com/12958.htm

University of Nebraska Board of Regents. (n.d.). Retrieved July 1, 2008, from http://www.sports-city.org/index.php

University reaps high five figures from Homecoming sponsorship. (2003). Retrieved November 17, 2003, from http://sponsorship.com/IEGR/2003/11/17/4710.asp

U.S. Paralympic Team. (2008). Retrieved September 15, 2008, from http://paralympics.teamusa.org

Veltri, F. (1996). Recognition of athlete-endorsed products. Paper presented at the Conference of the North American Society for Sport Management, Frederickton, NB.

VISA USA making the most of 2004 Olympic Games with marketing campaign. (2004, March 31) [Press release]. San Francisco: VISA USA.

Volvo and Sport Sponsorship. (1990, January 29). Special Events Reports, pp. 4–5.

Wells, J. (1996, June 10). The big money man. Macleans, 52–56.

Wilkinson, D. G. (1986). Sport Marketing Institute. Willowdale, Ontario: Sport Marketing Institute.

Williamson, E. (2004). Gulf States Toyota. Migala Report. Retrieved June 7, 2004, from http://www.migalareport.com/jun04_story2.cfm

Woodward, S. (2004, March 22–28). Allsate unveils HOF sponsorship. SportsBusiness Journal, 11.

World Wide Partners. (1999, January). Olympic Marketing Matters, 7.

Worldwide TOP Programme. (1998, January). Olympic Marketing Matters, 8.

Index

About the Author

Dr. David K. Stotlar teaches on the University of Northern Colorado faculty in the areas of sport marketing, sponsorship, and event management. He has had more than 60 articles published in professional journals and has written several textbooks and book chapters on sport management and marketing. He has made numerous presentations at international and national professional conferences. On several occasions, he has served as a consultant in sport management to various sport professionals and in the area of sport marketing and sponsorship, to multinational corporations and international sport managers. Dr. Stotlar was selected by the United States Olympic Committee as a delegate to the International Olympic Academy in Greece and the World University Games Forum in Italy and served as a venue media center supervisor for the 2002 Olympic Games. He has conducted international seminars in sport management and marketing for the Hong Kong Olympic Committee, the National Sports Council of Malaysia, Mauritius National Sports Council, the National Sports Council of Zimbabwe, the Singapore Sports Council, the Chinese Taipei University Sport Federation, the Bahrain Sport Institute, the government of Saudi Arabia, the South African National Sports Congress, and the Association of Sport Sciences in South Africa. Dr. Stotlar's contribution to the profession includes an appointment as Coordinator of the Sport Management Program Review Council (NASPE/NASSM) from 1999–2001. He previously served as Chair of the Council on Facilities and Equipment of the American Alliance for Health, Physical Education, Recreation and Dance and as a Board Member and later as President of the North American Society for Sport Management. Dr. Stotlar was a member of the initial group of professionals inducted as NASSM Research Fellows. He is also a founding member of the Sport Marketing Association.